Divine Healing Under the Searchlight

Divine Healing Under the Searchlight

Samuel Fisk

Regular Baptist Press
1300 North Meacham Road
Post Office Box 95500
Schaumburg, Illinois 60195

Library of Congress Cataloging in Publication Data

Fisk, Samuel.
    Divine healing under the searchlight.

    Bibliography
    1.   Faith-cure. I.   Title.
BT732.5.F53   615'.852   78-15083
ISBN 0-87227-057-2

CONTENTS

1

Introduction

At one time or another all of us experience sickness. No one is entirely free from pain. When these things touch us personally, we become more conscious of them. Physical suffering in its acute forms seems to press in upon one's very soul. His inmost being cries out.

How may these deep-felt experiences be explained? What should be our attitude? More particularly, does God's Word give any answers to these problems? Faced by such perplexities, the entire subject calls for forthright consideration.

The Issue Comes to the Fore

In the broad field of religious interests today, much emphasis is being given to social concern. The gospel, it is said, is intended to reach out to community improvement, reform efforts, the raising of economic standards among needy people. The earthly well-being of humanity is emphasized; care for the whole person is declared to be the church's responsibility.

From this it is only a step to the concept that the total man—spirit, soul and body—is the expected beneficiary of the evangel. We are not surprised, then, when there is much talk about "wholeness" in the redemptive process, meaning release from bodily ills as well as the meeting of spiritual needs. Anything short of that would seem to imply an unwarranted dichotomy.

If the gospel is for the whole man, the argument runs, then to stop with the salvation of the soul is to leave out a large portion of one's rightful heritage. Also it has been suggested that when the soul experiences the saving power of Christ, the release is so great that bodily well-being naturally follows. It is an inherent concomitant of what is to be received. Only one's failure to accept it, presumably, holds back the blessing.

In considering all this, the ramifications of the subject may be noted to cover a wide spectrum. And its adherents embrace many shades of view, ranging from those ranked with the more orthodox and sedate in manner to those who are emotionally demonstrative and less given to ordered usages.

POINTS NOT IN QUESTION

The issue before us is not whether God can heal the sick. Certainly our God is still the Almighty One. He is fully able to heal the body. As far as what God can do is concerned, He can immediately and completely heal anyone.

We affirm that God not only can, but on occasion does, heal sickness today in answer to prayer. We have seen it ourselves. We have found that in response to earnest, believing intercession on the part of His children, petitions are granted, including remarkable recoveries from illness. Most evidently, then, whenever bodily affliction strikes, it should be brought before the Lord. Prayer is eminently in order for all human needs.

The question, however, confronts us as to whether physical healing is in a special class, whether it should be expected more than miraculous working is expected in relation to other common needs for which one prays. Has God clearly said that certain things are always His will for His people?

Inquiring into what extent it is God's will to heal the sicknesses of His people raises no doubts as to either His wisdom or His love. Scripture fully assures us of both. But in regard to what may be God's invariable way of acting in a situation, the same source—Scripture—will have to give the answer.

We recognize without question that during Bible times the Savior and others—certain outstanding men of God—performed miracles of healing. The records of this are clear. We accept them at face value. No effort is made, as with the critics, to explain them away.

Having acknowledged the possibility of miraculous healings in our day, we will not make it our immediate purpose to investigate or evaluate particular cases. That would lead us far afield and involve us too deeply in the vagaries of claims and counterclaims. Likewise we refrain from commenting upon the work of particular individuals involved in healing movements or upon those centers where many assert healing may be found. That is hardly necessary for those willing to rest the case on the testimony of Scripture.

THE FINAL BASIS OF APPEAL

The endeavor to resolve any issue touching our religious life and practice can best be pursued by careful examination of the Scripture passages which may relate to it. An honest analysis of each reference to a subject in the Word of God will give a far better answer than could be gained by one's experience, by the testimony of others, by recourse to logic, or by any other source of appeal.

Under consideration in the present study, therefore, will be: What has God shown His will to be in relation to our bodily well-being? Is one justified in regularly expecting healing? Does one have a right to demand it? What is the measure of true faith in relation to these things?

We turn to the Bible. Various types of sickness and bodily illness are referred to in its pages. Miracles of healing were prominent in a number of periods of Bible history—although not in all. It is not necessary to examine every incidental Bible reference to physical ailments. No precept or directive applicable to us can be elicited from such scattered and minor allusions. Examination will be made of the best-known passages—those most frequently cited and upon which much emphasis has been placed in the area of what is commonly termed "divine healing."

Passages will be considered in the order of their occurrence in the Bible, beginning with the Old Testament. Where statements are cited or repeated in both Testaments, treatment will be presented under the Old Testament appearance.

Finally, the Scripture foundation having been surveyed, other related aspects of the subject will be reviewed.

2

OLD TESTAMENT PASSAGES CONSIDERED

Several Old Testament texts have commonly been quoted in relation to the well-known doctrine of divine healing. Before what seems to be implied in them is taken with finality, they should be given close examination. A striking phrase standing alone may not suffice to establish the full truth which seemingly is indicated by it. What do these passages really teach? How fully can we claim them in relation to our bodily needs? Let us pursue the inquiry with honest open-mindedness, ready to see and acknowledge truth wherever it may be found.

EXODUS 15:26: "I am the LORD that healeth thee."

The first Old Testament passage which should be examined is Exodus 15:26, a frequently quoted reference. The entire verse reads, "If thou wilt diligently hearken to the voice of the LORD thy God, and wilt do that which is right in his sight, and wilt give ear to his commandments, and keep all his statutes, I will put none of these diseases upon thee, which I have brought upon the Egyptians: for I am the LORD that healeth thee." The last part of this verse is most commonly quoted by itself, "I am the LORD that healeth thee." This phrase actually is one of the compound names of God, *Jehovah-ropheka*. Several things should be observed in order to understand the scope of this reference.

First, the promise was to the Hebrew people as they

emerged from bondage in Egypt. It was conditional for them. Being directly addressed to Israel, it was associated with the discipline of that nation. Going back a couple of verses, we read in verse 22, "So Moses brought Israel from the Red sea. . . ." In verse 24, "And the people murmured. . . ." Introducing what is before us, verses 25b and 26 appear, "There he [the Lord] made for them a statute and an ordinance, and there he proved them, And said, If *thou* wilt. . . ." The promise depended upon their response. "If thou wilt diligently hearken . . . and wilt do . . . and wilt give ear . . . and keep all. . . ." If the conditions were not met, the opposite would be true (as seen in Deuteronomy 28:60 and Amos 4:10). When we read of the wilderness experience of Israel, we wonder if any real number lived up to the high standard of obedience.

Secondly, for those who may possibly have met the conditions, the promise was, "I will put none of these diseases upon thee, which I have brought upon the Egyptians." Israel had just passed through the plagues of Egypt and had come out of that land. The diseases referred to had been put upon the Egyptians in the form of judgments for resistance to the will of God. The promise involved what had occurred under those circumstances. The Israelites would not be confronted with that situation as long as they were true to Jehovah.

A similar promise was given to Israel in Exodus 23:25, "I will take sickness away from the midst of thee." The word translated "diseases" in 15:26 is the same word here rendered "sickness." The same conditions as in chapter 15 are put upon this promise in chapter 23. Beginning with verse 21, we find "obey . . . provoke him not . . . obey . . . do all. . . ." Verses 23 and 24 speak of being brought into the land of the Canaanites who were to be "cut off" and whose idols should be destroyed, a promise limited to Israel in the land. (Compare similar promises in Leviticus 26:16, 21; Deuteronomy 7:15; 28:60, 61.)

Another significant thing should be seen here. The Lord says in Exodus 15:26, "I will put none of these diseases upon thee, which *I have brought* upon the Egyptians." Sickness, therefore, does not always come from Satan. Here the Lord brought sickness upon certain ones, and it was for a purpose. It cannot be said that Satan is always the author of sickness. Nor can it be said that if Jesus died to destroy the works of the Devil, therefore He died to abolish sickness. Other allusions to sickness being sent of God, either directly or indirectly and for a purpose, are seen in Genesis 12:10-20; Exodus 32:35; 2 Samuel 12:15; 2 Kings 15:5; 2 Chronicles 21:18; John 9:2, 3; 11:4.

Did the nation of Israel reap the benefit of this promise as given in Exodus 15:26? As to deliverance from sickness, there are no records of immunity from sickness or of miraculous healing through the periods that followed: the times of Joshua and the conquest of the land; the period of the Judges; the reigns of Saul, David and Solomon; or the early days of the Divided Kingdom. Not, apparently, until the days of Elijah did supernatural healings occur. Not that people were spared sickness through all this time, but it seems that amid their changing fortunes, sickness and disease reaped its ordinary harvest. It may be noted that sanitary provision had to be made for lepers and sufferers from other bodily afflictions. (For further evidence of the continuance of sickness, see 1 Samuel 19:14; 1 Kings 14:1; 15:23.)

The passage in Exodus 15, therefore, cannot be quoted as ground for deliverance from sickness. Taken in its fuller context, it had reference to something quite special or restricted. Human mortals generally, including true believers, are subject to the ordinary frailties of the flesh.

PSALM 103:3: "Who healeth all thy diseases."

This is another frequently cited text. To be properly understood, this verse must be taken in the light of grammatical construction and Hebrew literary usage.

When "thy diseases" is mentioned, to whom does "thy" refer? The antecedent is in verses 1 and 2: "my soul." Thus the soul's diseases—rather than those particularly of the body—are in view in this familiar passage.

This text may be compared with Psalm 41:4 where the psalmist prays to the Lord: "Heal my soul; for I have sinned." Healing is applied to the soul and is associated with sin.

Psalm 103:3 likewise brings up the sin problem: "Who forgiveth all thine iniquities." The text speaks of the spiritual needs of the sin-weighted soul. The entire verse reads, "Who forgiveth all thine iniquities; who healeth all thy diseases." This psalm begins and closes with the "soul" as the subject: "Bless the LORD, O my soul" (vv. 1a and 22b).

The term *soul* is sometimes taken in the sense of either the life or the entire animate existence. It is not merely the body. The word *body* could have been used if that had been primarily what was meant. The great majority of exegetes take the term *soul* in this psalm to refer to the spiritual life or to the soul as such.

This brings us to consider the nature of Hebrew literary style. The chief feature of its poetry is parallelism of thought, not rhyme as with us. This verse consists of two couplets. The second answers to the first, reiterating and strengthening it. The verse then could be rendered, "Who forgiveth all thine— the soul's—iniquities; who healeth all thy—the soul's— diseases."

Observe the *all* in each couplet. Just as the Lord forgives *all* the soul's iniquities, so He heals *all* the soul's diseases. If the second phrase is going to be applied to the body, then *all* the body's ills should be cured just as *all* one's sins are forgiven. Those citing this verse for divine healing should experience no exceptions. The second *all* cannot be limited to occasional ills any more than the first *all* can be restricted to God's forgiveness of only certain iniquities.

Some students, still believing that it applies to bodily heal- ing, take the statement of verse 3, "who healeth all thy dis- eases," in the sense that all true healing—with the use of medi- cal aids or without—comes ultimately from God, and that wherever any healing is found it is of the Lord. To this we can well agree.

A further examination of the context, however, confirms the spiritual sense found in these words. In verse 4 final or ultimate well-being is in view. When it says, "Who redeemeth thy life from destruction," the word *redeemeth* conveys the idea of the judicial aspects of sin's ransom. The word for "destruc- tion" is frequently translated "the pit" in modern versions. This is the underworld of the dead, that realm from which we are redeemed.

Verse 5 says, "Who satisfieth thy mouth with good

things." If people would claim that statement in the same way they say they have a right to claim bodily healing, they would cease from toil and the common means of gaining a livelihood. But if we do not expect miraculous provision for bodily sustenance, we have no more right to expect it for diseases which touch the body. We pray for our daily provision, trust the Lord and do our part. We should treat equally and consistently the various aspects of the one (healing) as of the other (daily livelihood).

Verse 5 goes on, "So that thy youth is renewed like the eagle's." These phrases relate to us in the sense that all good things come to us from the Lord, and we praise Him for all. But we do not tell the infirm aged that they should be perpetually renewed in youth so that they will never know the limitations of old age. Yet this should be the case if complete bodily well-being, based upon this passage, were in view.

This Scripture goes much too far for divine healing advocates to rest comfortably. *All* diseases are mentioned. Leaders in healing meetings often wear glasses and show evidence of using modern dentures, to say nothing of their resorting to drugstore remedies on occasion. Yet they will quote "healeth *all* thy diseases."

If the text were taken literally, it would, of course, include even those final illnesses from which nearly everyone, sooner or later, succumbs and departs from this world. It would be an amazing testimony if some particular group of believers never suffered from any diseases, if they stood apart in being quite free from the common ills which afflict the rest of humanity. We have never heard of such a group, and yet that is what we should expect if this verse was practiced as advocated.

Outstanding hymn writers have grasped this Scripture truth and have set forth the healing of the soul from sin's deep wounds. Charles Wesley put it:

> Jesus, the sinner's Friend, to Thee,
> Lost and undone, for aid I flee. . . .
> Pity and heal my sin-sick soul;
> 'Tis Thou alone canst make me whole.

The saintly divine Philip Doddridge expressed it:

> He comes, the broken heart to bind,
> The bleeding soul to cure,
> And with the treasures of His grace,
> T' enrich the humble poor.

Even blind Fanny Crosby could sing:

> Trusting only in Thy merit,
> Would I seek thy face;
> Heal my wounded, broken spirit,
> Save me by Thy grace.

Johnson Oatman's words should be familiar:

> There's not a friend like the lowly Jesus—
> No, not one! no, not one!
> None else could heal all our soul's diseases—
> No, not one! no, not one!

Finally, these words movingly convey the thought:

> There is a Balm in Gilead
> To make the wounded whole;
> There is a Balm in Gilead
> To heal a sin-sick soul.

ISAIAH 53:4: "He hath borne our griefs [sicknesses]."

Two adjoining verses in Isaiah 53 are much relied upon by those claiming that Christ's sacrificial work provides for bodily healing. They are Isaiah 53:4 and 5. Each one is referred to in a separate book of the New Testament, and these references must be considered; so we will look at the verses individually.

The first half alone of Isaiah 53:4 is commonly quoted: "Surely he hath borne our griefs, and carried our sorrows." In the American revision of 1901 we find the same rendering in the text, but a footnote suggests the alternate rendering of "sicknesses" for "griefs." And "sicknesses" has found its way into the text of some modern translations. In a few translations "pains" has been substituted for "sorrows." These possible renderings have led bodily healing advocates to seize upon this passage as proof that Christ's dying work provides for our physical needs as well as our spiritual. But in this viewpoint several things have been overlooked.

In the first place, while the Hebrew word for "griefs" in Isaiah 53:4 may be rendered "sicknesses," that is not the invariable or only possibility. If it had been, the older revisers would not have used "griefs." In Jeremiah 10 the prophet refers to the casting out of the inhabitants of his beloved land (v. 18). Feeling it so deeply, he says, "This is a grief [same word], and I must bear it" (v. 19). Here "grief" is undoubtedly the most valid rendering of this term. The same expression is found in Jeremiah 6:7.

Even if "sickness" is considered the primary meaning, the Bible writers frequently use sickness in a figurative or symbolic manner to represent sin, disobedience, rebellion or the moral consequences thereof. To be sure, Isaiah himself uses it this way. In Isaiah 1:5 he says, "The whole head is *sick*, and the whole heart faint," referring to the "sinful nation, a people laden with iniquity," having "forsaken the LORD" (1:4); and to "your country" being desolate (1:7). Thus sin-sickness is often the main thing in view.

The next major fallacy in the use of this text relates to the time when Christ fulfilled it. Whether the allusion is to physical needs or otherwise, its New Testament usage plainly shows that it was fulfilled in the earthly ministry of our Lord—in His sympathetic and healing ministrations *before* the cross. That would indicate that it was temporary and was not associated with His enduring atonement on Calvary.

Matthew quotes these words of Isaiah near the beginning of Jesus' healing ministry. Matthew says that the statement was *fulfilled* there. The record is, "When the even was come, they brought unto him many that were possessed with devils: and he cast out the spirits with his word, and healed all that were sick: That it might be fulfilled which was spoken by [Isaiah] the prophet, saying, Himself took our infirmities, and bare our sicknesses" (Matt. 8:16, 17). This is how God says the words of Isaiah were fulfilled—over two years before the crucifixion.

But someone may raise the point that Isaiah 53 graphically sets forth Christ's great sacrificial work in His crucifixion. Therefore all that it involves must be included in His death. This would show that He died for both the physical and spiritual needs of men.

However, while the crucifixion is prominent in that chapter, other elements of His life are also seen. In fact, the cross comes into view beginning with verse 5. Verse 2 speaks of how He would "grow up." He was "despised and rejected" (v. 3) well before the crucifixion (Mark 5:40; Luke 4:28, 29; Matt. 13:58). The last verses of Isaiah 53 refer to Christ's exaltation. Thus every verse in that chapter does not find its fulfillment in what Christ did upon the cross.

The questions may arise: If the words of Isaiah 53:4 found fulfillment in Jesus' healing others, was that really bearing or taking upon Himself their sicknesses? And if, as suggested, the "sicknesses" quite possibly referred to moral and spiritual ills, how would curing physical maladies fulfill that? Both questions may be answered by saying that outstanding students of the Word hold that the great mainspring of Jesus' healing ministry was His facing the people's griefs and sorrows, His entering into and carrying those outworkings of their sad spiritual state in sympathy and compassion. The healings were an outward evidence of this.

ISAIAH 53:5: "With his stripes we are healed."

The second statement from Isaiah 53 commonly quoted in relation to our subject is the last phrase of verse 5, "And with his stripes we are healed." Since these words occur twice in Scripture, neither verse should be considered without reference to the other. In 1 Peter 2:24 the New Testament meaning and application are given.

Many aspects of the Savior's work are brought out in Isaiah 53, but verse 5 and following have special reference to His sufferings in His crucifixion. Careful attention to this shows that He was "wounded for our transgressions"—not for our bodily ills; He was "bruised for our iniquities"—not for our physical diseases. Our spiritual redemption is in view here. Other verses in the chapter reiterate this. His suffering was for our iniquities (v. 6); it was for our transgressions (v. 8); He was made an "offering for sin" (v. 10). Thus the healing by His stripes must refer to the healing of our sin-burdened souls.

This is exactly the way Peter applies it in his epistle. In 1 Peter 2:24 we read: "Who his own self bare our SINS in his own body on the tree, that we, being dead to SINS, should live unto righteousness: by whose stripes ye were healed." There is no reference whatever to bodily illness in this verse.

As these statements in Isaiah and 1 Peter are compared, it is striking to note that the very next verse in each case is parallel and helps give the meaning. Isaiah 53:6 speaks of our being "like sheep," having "gone astray." First Peter 2:25 speaks of our having been "as sheep going astray," but now being returned to the Shepherd of our "souls." Note that word *souls.* Bodies are not the principal thing in view here. Indeed, in His stripes there is healing for the "soul."

The Greek word for "healed" employed by Peter in the phrase "by whose stripes ye were healed" is the same as that used in Luke 4:18, "He hath anointed me to preach the gospel to the poor; he hath sent me to *heal* the brokenhearted, to preach deliverance to the captives. . . ." Healing the brokenhearted most certainly refers to men's spiritual needs. This also was drawn from Isaiah. He speaks of the Savior being sent "to bind up the brokenhearted, to proclaim liberty to the captives. . ." (61:1). This was fulfilled by Christ, but obviously in a spiritual sense.

If all were to be strictly literal, where during His earthly ministry did He effect "deliverance to the captives" or "set at liberty" anyone bound? He would have had an excellent opportunity to do this in the case of John the Baptist. But even when that noble character's plight was called to His attention, He deliberately did not effect any release. Nor do we see Him setting actual captives free nowadays. To claim this text in the literal manner, we should see such things commonly occurring today, and healing of the body should be no more demanded than this. Obviously the reference is to the captivity of men's souls to sin; and the "setting at liberty" has reference to release from the power of Satan, the enemy of souls.

The Greek word for "healed" used by Peter and Luke is used in additional places for other than physical healing. Three times it occurs in reference to the people's hearts and to their spiritual conversion: "This people's heart is waxed gross . . . lest at any time they should . . . understand with their heart, and should be converted, and I should *heal* them" (Matt. 13:15).

(See also John 12:40 and Acts 28:27.) These all reflect back to Isaiah 6:10.[1]

One more thing should be noted before leaving 1 Peter 2:24. In citing the words from Isaiah 53:5, the apostle was evidently led by the Spirit to alter the tense of the verb. Isaiah says, "With his stripes we are healed." Peter says, "By whose stripes ye were healed." Isaiah speaks prophetically of Jesus' saving work as it was being accomplished. Peter, writing to believers after that event, looks back to the cross where his and their eternal redemption was won. We cannot presume that all those to whom Peter wrote (and in the providence of God it includes us) were healed of all their physical ills. Yet this is what would be required if the statement is taken literally, for he says "ye were healed." But being saved, their souls having found peace at the cross, it is quite true that they "were healed" spiritually, and only in that way were they all healed. Thank God that we, too, regardless of our physical state, can look back to Calvary and say that our souls were healed there.

NOTE:

1. Dr. Rowland V. Bingham goes so far as to say, "As a matter of actual fact, every time Isaiah uses the word 'health' or 'healing' he has spiritual and not physical health or healing in mind." He then gives as examples Isaiah 19:22; 30:26; 6:10; 57:17-19; 58:8 (*The Bible and the Body* [Toronto: Evangelical Publishers, 1921], p. 45).

3

NEW TESTAMENT PASSAGES EXAMINED

The witness of the New Testament may now be brought under review. Its extensive testimony will prove fully adequate for the purpose of our inquiry. The general aim will include negative and positive elements, showing where certain Scriptures do not apply and bringing out what is embraced in their true scope and meaning. The passages are discussed in the order of their appearance, a separate chapter being devoted to James 5.

MATTHEW 10:1, 7, 8:
"As ye go, preach . . . Heal the sick. . . ."

Jesus' giving His disciples authority to heal is frequently emphasized. We are told that this authority was never revoked. In that case we should expect the same works to be performed today. Examination of a familiar passage upon which such claims are based will prove helpful and show how similar references may be treated.

Of texts commonly appealed to, Matthew 10:1, 7 and 8 is a leading example: "And when he had called unto him his twelve disciples, he gave them power against unclean spirits, to cast them out, and to heal all manner of sickness and all manner of disease. . . . And as ye go, preach, saying, The kingdom of heaven is at hand. Heal the sick, cleanse the lepers, raise the dead, cast out devils: freely ye have received, freely give."

That anyone today would attempt to appropriate what is in

this passage is surprising. Three or four considerations, when forthrightly faced, show that we are outside the scope of what is involved here. All are found in the immediate context. Attention to the context is always a primary principle of sound Biblical interpretation.

First of all, this commission was specifically addressed to the twelve apostles and given only to them. Verse 1 says that Jesus "called unto him his twelve disciples," and He "gave them power." Then their names are carefully recorded (vv. 2-4) as the ones to whom the command was given and who fulfilled it at that time. Verse 5 says, "These twelve Jesus sent forth." Again, chapter 11 begins, "And it came to pass, when Jesus had made an end of commanding his twelve disciples, he departed. . . ." "The twelve" are most pointedly and repeatedly designated as the ones involved.

Second, verses 5 and 6, an essential part of this commission, distinctly limit the scope of the words. We do not hide behind a general dispensational casting aside of most of what is in the Gospels, but the very words here say, "Go not into the way of the Gentiles . . . But go rather to the lost sheep of the house of Israel." This indicates a limited commission of immediate significance to the people of Israel. We Gentiles are wholly outside of it. Further evidence of this limitation is seen in verse 23, "Ye shall not have gone over the cities of Israel, till the Son of man be come." The account relates that these disciples then went on just such a mission to the cities of Israel and returned to the Lord before He ever had been crucified for the world's sin.

Third, the context reveals the peculiar circumstances of the times. "Provide neither gold, nor silver, nor brass in your purses" (v. 9). Even their clothing was to be sharply restricted (v. 10). It was a quick mission on which they were sent at that particular time. Purely Eastern customs were to be followed, as the shaking off of the dust from their feet if they were not received (v. 14). If the words about disregarding gold and silver were followed today, we believe we would see less effort displayed by certain individuals to become known as divine healers!

The fourth consideration showing the inapplicability of

this commission to us is found in verse 8, imbedded in the middle of the words so commonly quoted for practice today. I heard Aimee Semple McPherson quote this text in this manner: "Heal the sick, cleanse the lepers, cast out devils: freely ye have received, freely give." The words "raise the dead" were conveniently omitted. I should say, deliberately the words were omitted. That is handling the Word of God deceitfully, wresting the plain words of Scripture. Others have followed the same pattern in quoting the text. They could well blush with shame, admitting that here they must, of necessity, fail. Either the words of Jesus should be followed as a pattern, or they should not. The words should all be taken or not be taken at all.

When raising the dead is mentioned, sometimes the claim is made that in some cases the dead actually have been raised. But, admittedly, these cases are rather rare. We have heard of such exceptional instances. The latest to come to my attention are some alleged raisings of the dead amidst recent stirrings in Indonesia.

But these instances defeat the very claims they are expected to uphold. The fact that they are rare or exceptional proves that these words taken as a whole cannot be ground for what is expected as a regular practice in the Christian Church. If the healings, along with the raisings of the dead, recorded in the New Testament are to be the rightful lot of God's people generally, why are they not commonly witnessed? Should not the raising of a dead body be claimed with just as much assurance as is the healing of a body? Instead, appeal is made to something observed by very few firsthand witnesses. Do we have to base the claim of a practice intended for us on something which we must go to far off Indonesia to substantiate? The whole thing breaks down. Let only those in some place such as Java profess to be following the pattern Jesus left.

Jesus raised the dead, as far as specific accounts go, three times. And the apostles (aside from what may have grown out of the occasion here considered) in only a few instances. These raisings were all well attested. Not only was the evidence of each death unquestioned, but also large numbers of both believers and unbelievers could bear witness to what was wrought. In the case of Lazarus, who had been dead four days, *many* came from the city to see him (John 12:9-11). Truly, "this thing was not done in a corner" (Acts 26:26), and neither should the evidences (?) of miracles today be so. In apostolic days even those who were hostile had to admit "that indeed a notable miracle hath been done by them is manifest to all . . . and we cannot deny it" (Acts 4:16). The warning of Matthew 24:26 well applies here: "Wherefore if they shall say unto you, Behold, he is in the desert; go not forth: behold he is in the secret chambers; believe it not."

Once more, note that the context indicates that Jesus empowered His twelve disciples "to heal *all* manner of sickness and *all* manner of disease" (Matt. 10:1). There were no limitations. No human ill was outside the range of what they were to overcome. Nothing suggests that faith was requisite on the part of those who benefited. Similarly there should now be no exceptions, no conditions, no failures, no turning away from surmounting every human ill.

Some have asserted that the reason more works such as raisings of the dead are not seen today is because of our general lack of faith or because we have gotten so far away from a faith which is simple and unsophisticated. In the few places in the world where the faith is fresh, childlike and uncluttered, it is declared such miracles occur. However, we find no Biblical ground for these assertions. When Jesus raised the son of the widow of Nain, no one before or at the time exercised any kind of faith as far as the record goes. When Peter raised Dorcas (Tabitha, Acts 9:36-42) the believers, rather than exercising faith that something overcoming death would occur, stood by "weeping" (v. 39), assuming it was all over. In Matthew 10 when Jesus sent forth the disciples on their early mission, no expression is given to the thought that faith would be requisite or expected on the part of those dealt with.

We are not denying that in rare cases God may be working in such supernatural ways today. God is sovereign; He can and may on occasion do the exceptional. But the exceptional, or the more or less hidden, is no sound foundation to back up claims of miracle-working by men today. The rare and exceptional (if it can be authenticated) is no proof that what is alluded to in Scripture is now finding complete fulfillment.

MARK 16:18: "They shall lay hands on the sick, and they shall recover."

A passage frequently cited in connection with the claims of divine healing is Mark 16:17, 18 and 20: "And these signs shall follow them that believe; In my name shall they cast out devils; they shall speak with new tongues; They shall take up serpents; and if they drink any deadly thing, it shall not hurt them; they shall lay hands on the sick, and they shall recover. . . . And they went forth, and preached every where, the Lord working with them, and confirming the word with signs following. Amen."[1]

These words were spoken by the Lord in connection with His charge to His disciples to go forth and preach the gospel (vv. 15, 16). Several things need to be noted here.

First, five things, it was said, would be manifest by those to whom the words apply. The words "they shall speak with new tongues" and "they shall lay their hands on the sick" are often called to attention. The other three signs or miracles are just as frequently ignored. Rarely is the taking up of serpents practiced. And safely drinking a "deadly thing" is practically unknown in these days as far as we have heard.

Therefore, what casts doubt over the claims based upon these verses is the unwarranted selecting of one or two of these things according to one's inclination and entirely disregarding the rest. That is inconsistent and a misuse of the Word of God. We are not saying that if these words are to be fulfilled, one person must necessarily manifest all five signs. We only insist that if one or two of these things is for regular practice among Christians, so should the others be just as widely witnessed. If God's men today display one, such as healing, we should also see men of God commonly manifest the others.

If it be thought that these things are not all in the same category, this leads to observing that the signs were more specifically promised to those who founded the Christian Church. The words were directed to the apostles there present (v. 14). Verse 20 states, "They [those apostles] went forth, and preached every where," with the consequent "the Lord working with them" in miraculous ways.

The record shows that among the early apostles such signs were manifest; for example, the casting out of devils (demons or evil spirits; Acts 5:16; 8:7; 19:11, 12) and the taking up of deadly serpents with no ill effects whatsoever (Acts 28:3-6). Thus a number of these things were actually demonstrated by those upon whom Jesus personally laid such great responsibility.[2]

Note further that in this passage, these manifestations are twice referred to as "signs" (vv. 17, 20). It is natural to inquire, then, as to what kind of a sign or for what purpose. We are not left without an answer. Because they were specifically related to going and preaching, they were *confirming* signs. Verse 20 clearly says, "And they went forth, and preached every where, the Lord working with them, and confirming the word with signs following." At that time—the time of introducing a previously unknown faith into the world, and into a violently hostile Roman world—the signs served a unique purpose. The One Whom they were proclaiming was the despised and rejected One. Since He had manifest His credentials by miracles, those whom He personally selected and specially endued were likewise appointed to manifest certain special signs.

Some groups through the years have claimed apostolic succession, basing hierarchical or sacerdotal orders upon that concept. But evangelical believers have always resisted those claims, finding no warrant for them in Scripture. Likewise no sound warrant is found in Scripture for the passing on of these peculiar signs. In fact, just the opposite is indicated.

In Hebrews 2 these things are again referred to as confirming signs, applying only to those times. "How shall we escape, if we neglect so great salvation; which at the first began to be spoken by the Lord, and was *confirmed* unto us by them that heard him; God also bearing them witness, both with signs and wonders, and with divers miracles, and gifts of the Holy Ghost, according to his own will?" (Heb. 2:3, 4).

The writer of Hebrews was evidently not one of the original apostolic band. He says the word was "confirmed unto us [those who came after the twelve apostles] by them [the apostles] that heard him [the Lord]; God also bearing them [the apostles] witness, both with signs and wonders, and with divers miracles." All this was "according to his own will," that is, when and as it may have pleased Him, not as a regularly-to-be-expected thing. The writer does not indicate that second generation Christians had their own word confirmed to still others by any such signs and gifts.

God has wrought miracles through the centuries. We are not limiting omnipotence. We are only saying that a regular and continued practice of these things is not to be demanded on the basis of such passages as this in the Gospel of Mark.

JOHN 14:12: "The works that I do shall he do also."

The next text to examine is John 14:12. This text is frequently quoted by those supposing that healing miracles should be regularly experienced today. We have even heard Christian Scientists cite it in defense of their system. It reads: "Verily, verily, I say unto you, He that believeth on me, the works that I do shall he do also; and greater works than these shall he do; because I go unto my Father."

How surprising that such a text would be appealed to in defense of what is claimed as divine healing. Apparently this verse has not been carefully read; attention has not been given to all that it says; nor have its implications been thought through.

In the first place, Jesus said "he that believeth on me" shall do these works. Not he that has a special enduement, that receives a remarkable gift, that is singled out from the mass of believers or is called to some outstanding miracle-working vocation, but merely "he that believeth."

No doubt some will say, yes, it is available to all believers, but not all have the faith to claim it. But we go back to the text. It does not speak of those among believers who have certain necessary faith, nor those who will have the boldness to claim it. It just says "he that believeth on me." Whatever is involved should be realized by every believer in Christ.

Second, note that Jesus said both the same and "greater works" would be done. Two levels, therefore, are presented. If the reference is understood to be to Jesus' miracle works, we should see both the same and greater works performed.

Relate it first to the same works. We should see works of an equal nature being wrought today. Where are multitudes of five thousand or more being miraculously fed? Nothing indicates that the "works" are limited to healings. Where is water being instantly transformed into wine? Where do we see people walking across the surface of a stormy sea? (That would be a great boon to missionaries.) And where are the dead being immediately raised from the grave?

Then Jesus also said "greater works" would be done. Very well, where are works being performed that surpass those which Jesus did? If He fed five thousand, we should see tens of thousands miraculously fed. (No worry about famine in India.) As He calmed the Sea of Galilee in a moment, we should see cyclones or hurricanes stopped in their tracks. Jesus healed "all" the afflicted who crossed His path (Matt. 4:23, 24; 9:35; 12:15; Luke 4:40; 6:17-19). We should see entire hospital wards emptied and sanatoriums abandoned. Three times Jesus raised the dead to life. To surpass that we should see all those in the city morgue come to life. What a demonstration! We could even hope to see graves emptied. People would think the final day of judgment had come. Obviously something is wrong here. Let no one say we are distorting the picture. We are only taking it literally—as we are told that it should be taken.

What, then, is the meaning? The text itself gives the answer. Observe the last phrase of the verse. It is usually overlooked, but it gives the key to understanding the whole. Jesus said that these and greater works would be done "because I go unto my Father." What was dependent upon His going to His Father? In this same Upper Room Discourse we read, "Nevertheless I tell you the truth; It is expedient for you that I go away: for if I go not away, the Comforter will not come unto you; but if I depart, I will send him unto you" (John 16:7). The coming of the Holy Spirit, then, was what was involved. Indeed, in 16:10 He goes on to say that the Spirit will convict the world of righteousness "because I go to my Father."

This is borne out in John 14:16 and 17. Jesus says He will "pray the Father, and he shall give you another Comforter . . . even the Spirit. . . ." (See also John 14:26 and 15:26 and 27.) Thus the works of the Holy Spirit in and through His followers are the greater works of which Jesus spoke. Jesus' earthly ministry reached but a few, principally Israelites. But soon a great harvest of Gentile souls was to be brought in.

Since Jesus accomplished the superlative in physical miracles, and since these never have and apparently are not to be surpassed, the "greater works" are manifestly in another realm. The Holy Spirit indwells believers; and through believers' changed lives the world is convicted, lost men are witnessed to, and something greater than physical miracles is accomplished: salvation from sin is embraced and eternal life is found. Praise God! That is something which will last forever. Those physically healed by Jesus were still mortal and finally died. The fruit of this greater boon will never pass away!

ACTS 10:38:
"Healing all that were oppressed of the devil."

In this text the Devil is referred to. Demonism has become a subject of wide interest today. Demonic activity is nothing new in the world. Even Jesus confronted these forces. Through Him alone could deliverance be effected. But it is pertinent to ask how far and in what areas these satanic efforts are directed.

Two or three phrases of Scripture have been associated in an attempt to build up a doctrine of healing. In Acts 10:38 we read that Jesus "went about . . . healing all that were oppressed of the devil." With these words might be coupled those of 1 John 3:8: "For this purpose the Son of God was manifested, that he might destroy the works of the devil." Also touching the subject is what was said of a woman whom Jesus healed: "Ought not this woman . . . whom Satan hath bound, lo, these eighteen years, be loosed from this bond?" (Luke 13:16).

Since Jesus healed the sick, and since certain subjects of healing were referred to as oppressed of the Devil, some people assume that bodily ills on the whole can be attributed to Satan. Since Jesus' confrontation with the work of the Devil consisted primarily in healing such Satan-inflicted sickness, they assume this healing work is His continuing goal. These are rather large assumptions.

The account in Acts 10 mentions healing those oppressed by the Devil. There is no direct reference in the passage to sickness or physical ills. Apparently not considered is that those so oppressed were not merely people with ordinary sickness;

they were more particularly afflicted with demons or possessed of evil spirits. Often Jesus' healing consisted of casting out devils (demons) and delivering the ones so oppressed. In some instances physical ills accompanied or were the result of demon possession. When the evil spirits were cast out, both spiritual soundness and physical health resulted. (See, for instance, Matthew 8:16; 9:32, 33; Luke 4:36; 8:2.)

Considering the broader aspect of things, the same word for "healing" in Acts 10:38 is frequently used in relation to other than physical ills: Matthew 13:15; Luke 4:18; John 12:40; Acts 28:27; Hebrews 12:13. This could show that the reference to Jesus' "healing" may well have gone beyond physical cures.

As to Satan being the source of physical sickness, we have already seen that Satan is not the sole originator of bodily affliction. Some sickness may be attributable to Satan; some may be an instrument of God; and some may come from natural causes, such as violating common health principles.

Furthermore physical affliction is not Satan's only or his chief modus operandi. Without a doubt he is more concerned with the souls of men than with their bodies; he more frequently uses spiritual weapons than physical. As the Word clearly indicates, ". . . Stand against the wiles of the devil. For we wrestle *not* against flesh and blood, but against principalities, against powers, against the rulers of the darkness of this world, against *spiritual* wickedness in high places" (Eph. 6:11, 12).

Satan's prime activity is the battle for the souls of men. When the word of the gospel is sown, "then cometh the devil, and taketh away the word out of their hearts, lest they should believe and be saved" (Luke 8:12). (See also 2 Corinthians 4:4; 1 Thessalonians 2:18; Luke 22:31; Matthew 13:38, 39.) Is it not sound to conclude that Jesus' chief concern is to meet and triumph over Satan's chief and most dangerous work?[3]

The context of the passage in Acts 10 confirms all this. The words about healing those "oppressed of the devil" were part of Peter's sermon in the house of Cornelius. The conclusion was not a concern for healing bodies. Rather, Peter says, "He commanded us to preach unto the people, and to testify that it is he which was ordained of God to be the Judge of quick and dead

. . . that through his name whosoever believeth in him shall receive remission of sins" (vv. 42, 43). Thus "sins" and the preaching of that which will bring remission are given the highest priority. Having referred to Jesus' healing, Peter did not conclude his sermon by giving special directives to those with bodily ailments.

In this light how mistaken is the assumption that "oppression of the devil" refers only to physical sickness. Satan binds in more than one way, and his great goal is always the destruction of the souls of men.

Also we should recognize that Jesus' healing "all that were oppressed of the devil" (or casting out evil spirits from those oppressed) was part of His preliminary, pre-crucifixion ministry—His credentials—just as was His feeding of the multitudes, walking on the water, and calming the storm. These all served to pave the way for the recognition and acceptance of His great work of dying for the sins of the world.

ACTS 14:9: "He had faith to be healed."

When Paul and Barnabas were in Lystra, they found a cripple who had never walked. "Perceiving that he had faith to be healed," he was commanded to stand. The result was immediate and complete healing. The phrase in Acts 14:9 seems to indicate that faith on the part of the afflicted is a requisite for healing, or that anyone with adequate faith may be healed.

The case of the blind men in Matthew 9 is similar. Jesus asked them, "Believe ye that I am able to do this?" Upon receiving an affirmative answer, Jesus said, "According to your faith be it unto you," and they were healed (Matt. 9:28-30).

Such incidents are now given as proof that faith on the part of the suffering one is an essential element of healing. If the healing is not found or if it later fails, the fault is laid at the door of the sick one's lack of faith. Thus the healer avoids responsibility.

True, in certain instances healing appeared to be in response to faith. However, this was by no means always the case. And even where faith was present, there is no proof that healing might not have taken place anyway, without the faith. On many occasions healing was brought about where it is evident that there was no faith, or in spite of the lack of faith. Some who were healed by Jesus did not know who He was when the healing occurred. And some whom the apostles healed had never before heard of Christ (e.g., Acts 28:8, 9). Thus in Acts 14:9 Paul healed where there was faith. But this is the only place in Acts where faith is mentioned in connection with healing.

As an example of healing without faith in Christ, consider the lame man whom Jesus healed at the pool of Bethesda (John 5:1-15). In verse 7, after Jesus had spoken to him, the cripple expressed no hope of being cured, only despair. Then, after being healed, when he was asked who had been responsible for it, he said he did not know who had healed him (v. 13).

John 9 gives the account of the healing of the man born blind. After his recovery, his lack of faith in the Savior is shown by his saying that he did not know whether the One opening his eyes was a sinner or not (v. 25). Later, when Jesus found him and asked him if he believed on the Son of God, he inquired who that was (vv. 35, 36).

Jesus healed some even when there appeared to be protest against it (Matt. 8:28, 29; Mark 1:23-26). In one instance, one who evidently was an unbeliever and with the enemies of Jesus was healed (the high priest's servant, Luke 22:51).

Several times, to be sure, Jesus said to someone, "Thy faith hath saved thee," or, "Thy faith hath made thee whole." Of course, the Lord always wanted to encourage faith, and He commended it when it was present. Some may have been healed in response to faith, but many were cured in spite of the absence of it. With some, the faith followed the healing.

Yet, in spite of all this, we are told that just as salvation is found only by faith in Christ, so healing is found only by a similar exercise of faith.

Rather than depending on the seeker's faith, the responsibility for faith rested upon those who ministered to the needy. In a notable case, Jesus rebuked His disciples for *their* lack of faith when they could not cure the son of a deeply burdened man (Matt. 17:14-20). Similarly, as will be seen in James 5, it is the faith of those who pray over the sick one which is effectual, not the faith of the suffering individual.

How tragic in the light of the full truth, how cruel to tell some deeply afflicted person that his healing is not forthcoming or has failed because he did not have the proper faith. And how unlike anything we find in Scripture.

All this does not rule out the possibility that in some cases the Lord may lay it on the heart of an individual to take his need to God in prayer. He may place his confidence in the prayer promises of the Word and look to God in faith to grant recovery from sickness. But it might not come in the same way for another individual, or even come similarly to this individual on another occasion. No assurance can be found for invariable healing among believers, faith or no faith.

ROMANS 8:11:
"He . . . shall also quicken your mortal bodies."

A common example of a text misunderstood in relation to bodily healing is Romans 8:11. It should not require extensive treatment, for a candid examination of what is said will show it does not refer to that which has so frequently been supposed.

The whole verse reads, "But if the Spirit of him that raised up Jesus from the dead dwell in you, he that raised up Christ from the dead shall also quicken your mortal bodies by his Spirit that dwelleth in you." The assumption is that to quicken your bodies means to give them present physical well-being. Attention to the precise wording of the text and to the main theme of the passage will clarify the meaning of the phrase in question.

In the first part of the verse, the mighty Spirit of God is related to the bodily resurrection of Christ. The same Spirit Who played so vital a part in that resurrection is an instrument to the same end in behalf of believers. He will raise their bodies from the dead.

The old English word *quicken* means to "make alive" or "raise up," as it is rendered in practically every version since King James' day. The ultimate resurrection body will be far in advance of our present bodily state. It will be a glorified, vitalized body free from infirmities, pain and such limitations as we are sure to know down here. That is something to anticipate with joy.

The word *also* in the text underscores this, for it means that as Jesus was raised, so also we shall be raised. Since Jesus was not healed of any physical sickness, neither can it refer to our bodily illnesses. Note further that the "shall also quicken," or make alive, is in the future tense, not present. Thus the reference is to the future resurrection of the believer's body, not to some passing deliverance from present bodily infirmities.

Additional indications referring this to a future resurrection are found in this same chapter. Verse 17 states that we are heirs of God. Our inheritance, though sure, is far from complete while we are sojourners down here. Verse 17 then says, "If so be that we suffer with him"—and we commonly do here—"we may be also glorified together." Future tense again. Our glorification awaits the resurrection when we shall have glorified bodies. Verse 18 puts it all in the future, "the glory which shall be revealed in us."

Verse 19 says that the creature "waiteth" for this manifestation. Verse 21 says that the creature "shall be delivered"—future tense once more—from that which is subject to corruption. This is far different from claiming present release from debilitating infirmities.

Then verse 23 caps it all by directly stating that we wait for the adoption, that is, for "the redemption of our body." This should finalize the matter. We have not the redemption of the body now, but we are waiting for it. We "hope" for it, and "with patience wait for it" (vv. 24, 25). It would seem that those who are demanding it for the present have abandoned the patience of which Scripture speaks.

However, for any who might yet feel that for us weary pilgrims there is some present encouragement in Romans 8:11, it would not so much indicate healing from sickness as being enlivened or exhilarated by the Spirit of God for a life of praise, testimony and service. The indwelling Spirit can, to be sure, buoy us up, lift us above the clutches of sin and above our fears and discouragements. He enables us—while in our mortal bodies—to go forth as conquerors (v. 37) amid the antagonistic currents of this evil world. Praise God for such an outlook.

1 CORINTHIANS 12:9: "To another the gifts of healing."

A Scripture very commonly assumed to give evidence of the continuance of healing in the Church is 1 Corinthians 12:9

and 10: "To another [is given] faith by the same Spirit; to another the gifts of healing by the same Spirit; To another the working of miracles. . . ." This whole subject of the gifts of the Spirit has puzzled many. Are they still operative today, and where may they be found?

Our concern here is primarily with the matter of healing. Just what is referred to in this Corinthian passage? An answer will be found in the cumulative impact of several simple but important considerations.

1. The church at Corinth was a carnal, unspiritual church. While this epistle was intended for the instruction of the people of God through the centuries, yet the church at Corinth itself, as such, was not a church to be followed as an ideal. Paul upbraided this church more than any other church with which he had dealings.

2. While certain gifts are mentioned here, they are in general depreciated, and the more perfect way—love—is held up as the one supreme thing to be emulated (12:31—13:13). The Corinthians were berated for inordinate display of some of the things much sought after today, but this—love—is something never depreciated.

3. The matter of healing is not pinpointed as a gift, for the term always appears in the plural, "gifts of healing." Furthermore, 1 Corinthians 12 is the only place in the entire New Testament where it occurs. Paul wrote to many churches, yet made no mention of it to any other. Peter healed early in his ministry, yet Peter makes no mention of it in his two epistles. Nor is reference made to it by James, Jude or John.

4. Some of the gifts listed in this chapter are now greatly emphasized, blown up out of all proportion, to the exclusion— if not complete ignoring—of others. Why is this so? Where, today, are people who publicly claim the gift of "the word of wisdom," or "the word of knowledge" (v. 8), or the "discerning of spirits" (v. 10)? Such differentiation is not warranted when all is taken into consideration.

5. In this same epistle to the Corinthians Paul says of the believers that they "came behind in no gift" (1:7). This would include gifts of healing. The word for "gift" in this early statement is the same one *(charisma)* that is found in chapter 12.

They presumably would have had healing among themselves in no small measure since they were behind no one in possessing these things. In spite of this, Paul says of them, "Many are weak and sickly among you" (11:30). Many! Why was not the gift of healing exercised? The sick were their own brethren, members of the same assembly. Having the gift in large measure, why did those who possessed it not use it for their fellow believers who were in such need? Something is amiss here.

6. These gifts were manifest in the unparalleled apostolic days. The Church, something previously unknown, was just becoming established. Special demonstrations were evident during these infancy days of the Church. But the infancy characteristics were to be left behind (1 Cor. 13:11; 14:20). No passage of Scripture indicates that these gifts, including the gifts of healing, were to be permanent in the Christian Church. In two other epistles of Paul we read of gifts of the Spirit (Rom. 12 and Eph. 4), but in neither of these—nor in any other New Testament passage—are gifts of healing or of miracles included among the gifts.

7. First Corinthians 12, when read in the light of its larger context, deals with miraculous gifts or special workings, not what would be the ongoing order of things. The healings of the apostles were described as "miracles" (Acts 4:22; 8:5-7), "notable miracles" (Acts 4:16), "great miracles" (Acts 6:8), and "special miracles" (Acts 19:11). This quite undermines the widespread claims made today. The contention is that healing is normally to be expected by the people of God, that it was provided for in the atonement and therefore should regularly be claimed. That would not be miraculous or special healing; it is not what is referred to in the apostolic record.

These considerations rule out healing as a continuing gift of the Christian Church. The apostolic days of special demonstrations have passed. Whatever this was in Corinth, it is not something to be particularly sought or commonly expected.

HEBREWS 13:8: "Jesus Christ the same yesterday,
and to day, and for ever."

Hebrews 13:8 is frequently quoted by those claiming Jesus as our Healer. This text does not actually touch the matter of healing, nor does the context warrant its being pressed into service to that end. Appeal to it is thoughtless since no reference is made to bodily healing, miracle works, faith cures or anything of the like. Yet the words are repeatedly used in discussing these matters.

The reason the text is so quoted, of course, is because it is claimed that if Jesus could have and did heal the sick long ago, then being the same today, He can heal the sick now. Jesus certainly can heal the sick today; He is as able to perform miracles for the body's needs now as ever. The question is, Is this still His plan? Does this text imply that His ways or methods of action never change?

Being the omnipotent Son of God, Jesus can, as readily today as He once did, multiply loaves and fishes, turn water into wine, provide fish with coins in their mouths with which to pay taxes. Are any of these things still His way of working? If so, which ones? And if only certain ones, where are they singled out above the rest? If not thus singled out, we must conclude that all such miracle works are either to be continued alike or are equally in abeyance. If healing alone is considered, the question would still remain, Is it always His will for all of His children? Hebrews 13:8 does not say that it is.

It seems self-evident, as good reasoning would indicate, that somewhere we must qualify the statement of Jesus continuing the same. Christ is the same, but He is not still hanging on the cross; He is not still walking the dusty lanes of Galilee; He is not still working in the carpenter shop, rendering obedience to His earthly parents. Yet if the statement is going to be rigidly pressed, it could be made to fit any of these. Its arbitrary application is uncalled for.

While in His essential being and nature our Lord is ever the same, the Word of God tells us that His ways, though perfect, do change. "There are differences of administrations, but the same Lord" (1 Cor. 12:5). The time was when He smote with instant death those engaging in lying and deceit (Acts 5:1-10), but He no longer acts that way. (How different things might be if He still did!) He appeared in a glorious manifestation to His servant John on the Isle of Patmos, but He is not appearing to His servants that way today.

That the text does not apply to Jesus continuing a healing ministry as He did while here on earth should be evident from the context. Hebrews 13:3 reads, "Remember . . . them which suffer adversity, as being yourselves also in the body," or, as the Berkeley Version puts the last phrase, "as though you are suffering physically yourselves." Those in view were not chided for such physical ills, nor told that they should, through Jesus' unchanging ministry, claim deliverance from them. Rather than being rebuked, those who were so suffering were presented as an example to be followed.

Hebrews 13:8 goes too far for the use to which it is put. Of the past, present and future indicated in the text, the last term is not applied as are the first two. If Jesus exercises a ministry of healing bodies today as He did yesterday, will He continue exercising such a function throughout eternity? In eternity we will have resurrection bodies. The effects of the curse will be gone. We are specifically told that in that state "neither shall there be any more pain" (Rev. 21:4). Healing will be unnecessary. The popular use of this text breaks down. It becomes evident that the reference is to something very different.

What, then, is the meaning of the statement that our Lord is the same yesterday, today and forever? It is the divine nature in its essential attributes that never changes. Taken in the light of the context, the words also show that our Lord is the unchanging object of faith, that we should be encouraged to persevere amid trials and persecutions because He is the same to watch over and lend His presence to those who put their trust in Him—just as He did for the faithful in former days. The words are an exhortation to press on because of the unchangeableness of our Savior in His knowledge of and concern for His children. As He will forever display His deep love for them, so He will forever be the object of their praise.

Thank God for such a text, for the truth of an infinite Savior, unchanging in His love and compassion. But do not read into this text or any other that which is not there and which manifestly goes beyond God's revealed will for His children.

NOTES:

1. In some early manuscripts this passage is not included, and therefore has been considered inconclusive. Recognizing this unsettled point, we nevertheless treat it for its own sake.

2. No record is found in Scripture of drinking a "deadly thing," but we are not told all that the apostles did, just as we are told only a small portion of the sign-works which Jesus did (John 20:30; 21:25).

3. Beyond the damning of souls, or as an effort thereto—but still ahead of inflicting sickness—Satan aims to tempt people to evil, to entice them and draw them away from godliness (1 Thess. 3:5; 1 Tim. 3:7; 2 Cor. 11:3; 1 Cor. 7:5; Acts 5:3). In this sphere also, Christ's aim is to point the way of deliverance, far more essential than merely healing bodily ills.

4

JAMES 5 CONSIDERED

We are sometimes faced by those who want to know how fully we follow what is set forth in James 5 in respect to the sick. Do we hold to the Word of God? Or do we lack faith? Are we sidestepping a passage which is an essential part of the New Testament? The particular words in question are: "Is any sick among you? let him call for the elders of the church; and let them pray over him, anointing him with oil in the name of the Lord: And the prayer of faith shall save the sick, and the Lord shall raise him up" (James 5:14, 15).

How should these words be regarded? For help one may turn hopefully to the commentaries. But little assistance is found there. Older commentaries go to great lengths to demonstrate that this passage affords no ground for the Roman Catholic sacrament of extreme unction. To be sure the anointing with oil is not, as that church maintains, to prepare one for death. Just the opposite, it looks forward to the recovery of the sick. And it is not a priest, but the elders who are involved.

Some more recent commentaries have quickly passed over the passage, assuming that James was writing exclusively for Jews; or that the elders were individuals in the Jerusalem church of that day only; or that this was specifically one of the sign gifts which passed away with the completion of the New Testament. These points may satisfy some people. But can these things be positively established here in James? And if such considerations put the passage beyond us, could not the bulk of James' book similarly be passed by as not for the Church throughout this gospel age?

A more adequate answer and a scriptural answer, we believe, can be found by a full and close examination of the whole passage, facing it forthrightly.

A CLOSE LOOK AT THE PASSAGE

To begin with, these verses afford no encouragement for modern divine healers. It is not said that prominent individuals should call the sick to their places of meetings. Instead, the sick ones are to do the calling, and those who would minister to their needs are to go to them. Also, the sick are to call for the elders—plural—evidently the leaders of the church with which they are familiar. It does not involve some single person who has built up a reputation as a "healer," possessing a remarkable gift.

Furthermore, it is the prayer of faith of those who pray over the sick one which is given the emphasis; it is not the sick one's faith that counts. Failure of recovery cannot, as is so often done, be charged to lack of faith on the part of the afflicted.

Here let us say that we should most certainly pray for the sick. Prayer is the recourse of the believer at all times. We should put praying for the sick in the same class as praying for any and all of our needs. The promises of prayer cover health as well as the other issues of life. But the thrust of James 5 is to show, first, that afflictions may persist; secondly, that God's perfect will is manifest in different ways; and third, that we should be submissive to that all-wise divine will.

First, then, observe the recognition of affliction and the place God Himself may expect it to play in our lives. Verse 10 reads, "Take, my brethren, the prophets, who have spoken in the name of the Lord, for an example of suffering affliction, and of patience." Mark it: God's prophets were great men; they were holy and devout men; they were special instruments to execute His will. Yet we are told that they suffered affliction. Some of them suffered intensely, suffered prolonged affliction, suffered without visible relief. Are we better than they?

In verse 11 the patriarch Job is set forth as an example to us.

Job suffered, sought relief without avail, endured physical pain—and that for a purpose. He recovered only after that purpose was fulfilled. No doubt the lesson is that rather than seek a healer we should seek God's purposes in our ills.

With these examples as an introduction, the inspired account goes into the theme of the more commonly cited verses. But the context must not be overlooked. Let us get the full picture.

Pursuing this, part of the larger context also includes Elijah. As the verses just reviewed precede the texts in question, his case follows. Elijah wrought miracles. And the miraculous is sought today. However, has it been considered that only once did drought come at Elijah's hand, and apparently only once did he specifically pray for rain (vv. 17, 18)? That was God's plan, and God's purposes must be taken into account.

After the miraculous incidents referred to, Elijah had his own troubles and afflictions (threatened by Jezebel, fleeing, famished, despondent to the point of desiring death). We are no better than Elijah. But this seems evident: These incidents are placed before us to underscore the main theme of this whole section—patience amid affliction and committing all to God in prayer, seeking His perfect will.

Now we come to the verses of chief concern. In verse 13 the question is asked, "Is any among you afflicted?" The word *afflicted* is the same word which was used in verse 10 regarding the prophets who suffered affliction. Instead of any suggestion that they did or could have claimed deliverance and healing, those sufferers are presented to us as examples of patience under or along with their suffering. Verses 7 and 8 both begin with an exhortation to patience. Therefore, rather than teaching that healing is to be expected where faith is, this teaches that God may at times be glorified much more as the faithful show patience amid their suffering.

Next, consider the word *sick*. Verse 14 begins, "Is any sick among you?" *Sick* appears again in verse 15, but a different word is used. This latter occurrence could be rendered literally "to grow weary" (A.T. Robertson, *Word Pictures in the Greek New Testament*). The only other place where this term occurs in the New Testament is in Hebrews 12:3 where it is rendered "be wearied." This relates to the patience of verses 11 and 12. If God does not see fit to heal sickness, let us—in accord with the full teaching of this passage—ask Him to give us patience. As we do so, we believe He can give us peace in our souls along with the affliction.

THE ELDERS

Another question which naturally arises is, To whom does the designation "the elders" have reference? Some have supposed it refers to the apostles in the early church. But the original apostles would not be everywhere and at all times accessible. The epistle is addressed to certain ones "scattered abroad" (1:1). For believers so scattered it would be impossible for those apostles to be within easy reach, so this can hardly be the meaning. And of the regular successors of the twelve apostles (in their unique office) there is not the slightest evidence.

If the reference is to ordinary leaders in the local church, the presumption would be that they were fulfilling a regular function and not the special miracle-working power possessed by the apostles. But what regular function? In no other post-resurrection passage is any such function for elders set forth. The gifts of healing mentioned in 1 Corinthians are not related to elders, nor does that passage refer to the anointing we find in James.

It appears, then, that the only regular function in view is that of earnest, committed prayer. This always has a place.

THE USE OF OIL

If the intention was that some leaders of the local church follow this regularly when called upon by the sick, the question would still remain: Why was oil employed? What was the purpose of the anointing?

There seem to be four main possibilities as to the anointing with oil. (1) It was something limited to that time and not now fully comprehended; (2) it was for medicinal purposes; (3) it was a type or symbol; (4) it was a ceremonial rite. We will look at these in reverse order.

The Roman Catholic Church and a few others hold to the ceremonial or ritualistic use. If this be the case, then we have one more rite in the church, another ordinance. But as there is no record of such a rite in either the Book of Acts or in any other epistle, nor sufficient detail here in James to show clearly the employment of it as such a rite, we are led to reject this interpretation.

We also reject the suggestion that the oil is a symbol, possibly of the Holy Spirit. This would point to the Spirit working within us effecting the healing, or it would indicate that as healing benefits the body, so the Spirit benefits the soul.

In Old Testament symbolism, oil is acknowledged as a type (as in the anointing of the high priest and kings). But in following it through in the present passage, several essentials are lacking in this interpretation. The antitypical anointings with oil were for service or standing before God, not for physical well-being, and they were not for just anyone who wanted them. Since all true Christians have the Holy Spirit, if this anointing indicates the bestowal of something deeper than the initial Christian experience, where is an anointing of the Spirit set forth in this connection? And how is it related to bodily healing?

The ministry of the Holy Spirit is not part of the theme of James, and certainly not of this section where He is not even mentioned. If this stood for the Holy Spirit, then the elders employing it should look into the sick one's relation to the Spirit. But no such thing is anywhere suggested. There is no post-pentecostal reference to any symbolic meaning or use of oil in the apostolic church.

Consider the second interpretation, that the oil was used for its medicinal value. Larger commentaries give numerous examples of the belief that oil had healing properties. But if such a simple and common application was meant, why should the elders be called to come and apply it? Could not anyone in the family give it to the needy one? A recent commentary seriously suggests that James had in mind some bachelor who had no family members who could massage him with oil; so he had to call for the elders of the church to come and give him a rubdown! Poor fellow; perhaps he had not a single neighbor whom he could trust!

If medicinal use was what had been intended, modern religious practice would not comply with it. Only a fingertip—or at most a few drops—are employed, hardly sufficient to impart any medical benefit. On the other hand, with the development of medical science and modern remedies, any medicinal value would now be superceded, at least for most ailments.

Other minor interpretations of the oil have been suggested. One is that the oil is a sign of the miraculous healing which is expected or claimed. But there is no ground for this in James, the Gospels, Acts or any other epistle.

Another interpretation of the passage is that the instructions are to be applied only in limited cases where sickness is the result of unconfessed sin on the part of a believer. But how this is to be determined is not clear. Nor is the relation of the oil to confession apparent. Moreover, the text reads, "Is any sick among you?" The "any" would indicate no such limitation.

This brings us to the first view—that the reference is to something of significance appreciated in those times but now not fully comprehended. The end effect would be similar to that of the medical use—something out of vogue in our day. This would lead us to conclude that its purpose was fulfilled or that it was intended for a day now past. There has been much diversity of thought on the subject. Even scholars are unable to arrive at a consensus on any of the possibilities.[1] The allusion to this practice seems far removed from where we are today.[2]

If such anointing is not for us, why is it set forth in this epistle of practical exhortations? The answer has already been seen. It is in line with the example of Elijah in verses 17 and 18. We do not repeat his miraculous deeds, but he is held up as a model of prevailing prayer, an abiding example which we should emulate. The anointing with oil, like Elijah's miracles, is not the focal point, but the related praying is.

Any remedial measure we may now undertake (that of oil or otherwise) should be accompanied by faithful praying for God's blessing upon it and for God's perfect will to be done. If the anointing was associated with special miraculous power exercised in apostolic days, since prayer still played so large a part, the abiding lesson in that regard would come down to us just the same. Prayer and committing all to the will of God is the thrust of the teaching.

THE PRAYER OF FAITH

Correlating James 5 with similar words in James 1:5 and 6 has been largely overlooked. James 5:13 and 14 both begin with the words "Is any among you." James 1:5 begins with practically the same words, "If any of you lack wisdom, let him ask of God . . . and it shall be given him."

Apply the same principles in each case. We should pray for wisdom. God promises to give it to us. Does that mean we should never cultivate wisdom? Should we despise instruction or never go to school? Then why shrink from medical aids or bypass doctors? The one stands with the other. God is the great Giver, infinite and compassionate. Nevertheless we apply ourselves to wisdom, all the while asking for His enrichment, just as we apply health remedies and ask for His blessing upon them.

"Let him ask in faith, nothing wavering" (1:6) corresponds to "the prayer of faith" in chapter 5. We should always strive to pray in faith, believing. We have prayed for wisdom, but we do not claim to have received perfect and unceasing wisdom. So we pray in faith for the sick, trusting that God will do what is best for those in need. "The prayer of faith" quite evidently means trusting prayer, prayer offered in resignation to the will of God. It is the prayer of a trusting child, knowing as an earthly one would, that a wise and benevolent Father will grant the request if it is for the child's own good.

Sometimes the question is asked, Can we pray the prayer of faith for healing? To which we reply: To no greater extent than the apostle Paul did. Paul left his companion Trophimus sick at Miletum (2 Tim. 4:20). Did he pray the prayer of faith over him? Why, then, was Trophimus still ill? Paul advised Timothy to take something for his "stomach's sake and thine often infirmities" (1 Tim. 5:23). Why did he not recommend what is thought to be the scriptural means of help and have Timothy ask certain ones to pray the prayer of faith over him? Paul was deeply burdened for Epaphroditus who "was sick nigh unto death" (Phil. 2:27). But Paul did not say that he or anyone else prayed "the prayer of faith" over Epaphroditus to effect his recovery.

PRACTICAL ASPECTS

On a practical level, how should one respond if he is called upon to go and anoint and pray for the sick? The following course might well be followed.

First, the inquirer could be told that it would be most acceptable to have someone come and pray for the sick. It should be emphasized that confidence is placed in prayer in the will of God, but only that kind of prayer (James 4:15). (See also 1 John 5:14; Luke 22:42; Romans 1:10; 2 Corinthians 12:7-10.)

Second, an effort should be made to bring the afflicted one (or his loved ones, or both) to see the larger scope of this passage as has here been unfolded. Let a kindly and sympathetic attitude prevail, but let all that Scripture presents be insisted upon.

If anointing with oil is requested, ask why it is desired. The reply would probably be because it is mentioned in Scripture. The question could be further pressed, Why is it mentioned? For what purpose was it employed? This would give a better opportunity to explain the whole passage.

If anointing is still demanded, a Christian worker (or the elders) might decline on the basis of the practice being little understood. James is broadly recognized as the first book of the New Testament to be written. This being so, it would have set the standard of practice for all to follow. But apparently it was not a pattern to be regularly pursued, for no subsequent example of anything like this can be found in the New Testament.[3] Only the example of prayer remains.

Furthermore, it should be pointed out that this passage says prayer is to avail, not the anointing. And the concerned Christian stands ready to pray for the sick.

Some may insist, however, that the plain statement is that the prayer of faith "shall save the sick, and the Lord shall raise him up" (v. 15). Taken alone these words seem to leave no alternative other than the healing of the sick one. But the words should not be taken alone. It has already been shown that the context points to the prophets, men of faith, who suffered (v. 10), to Job whose faith was unshakable in the face of affliction (v. 11), and to faithful Elijah who was "a man subject to like passions as we are" (v. 17). Therefore, the passage itself, viewed as a whole, qualifies the range of what is presented.

Other prayer promises of the Word appear on the surface to be quite broad, but are always taken with commonly recognized limitations. In Mark 11:24 Jesus said, "Therefore I say unto you, What things soever ye desire, when ye pray, believe that ye receive them, and ye shall have them." In John 14:13 and 14, He said, "And whatsoever ye shall ask in my name, that will I do . . . If ye shall ask any thing in my name, I will do it." The *whatsoever* in these verses appears most sweeping. Some people apply such promises very specifically in the area of bodily healing, yet do not similarly claim them in other areas.

Outright unbelievers have been known to chide Christians, suggesting that if we took such statements at face value we could sit down and pray for quantities of money to appear before us, ask for an abundance of the good things of life to fall from the sky at our feet, and so on. But we all know, even with such broad promises to go on, that we do not so pray.[4] Why, then, put bodily healing in a special class, but nothing else? The promises of healing, like any others, must be taken with conditions or qualifications and with all that Scripture has to say on these subjects. Conditions of patience, trustfulness, endurance and resignation to the divine will must not be overlooked.

Incidents have occurred where good and godly men, men of real faith, have anointed with oil and prayed for the sick with no demonstrable change in the condition of those ministered to. On the other hand, in some incidents sincere men of God have anointed and prayed for sick ones, and healing, either gradual or in large measure, has followed. The latter examples may be held up as evidence of a seal of approval upon the practice in question. We would not depreciate any honest and well-intended effort. Yet who can say whether the answer in these latter cases might not have come just as surely by earnest prayer alone (without any relation to the employment of oil), or even that it may have come as a result of the ordinary curative processes of nature working in the body?

If we pray and leave it all with God in His infinite wisdom to do what He sees is right; if we are resigned to the purposes of Him Who knows better than we and Who may have ends in view which we do not now comprehend, then we may rest assured that we have done our part. Someday we will understand and see the larger plan of God in all of its perfection and beauty. Then we will only praise Him for His goodness and grace.

NOTES:

1. On this passage Arthur W. Pink says, "We are not sure in our own mind either as to its interpretation or application" (*Divine Healing* [Swengel, PA: Reiner Publications, n.d.], p. 20).

2. This may be regarded as in the same class as that referred to in a question presented to F. F. Bruce. The principle set forth is stated: "We are at a disadvantage here compared with the Corinthians. They knew what the apostle was speaking about, for it was they who asked the question. . . . But we are in the position of people listening to one end of a telephone conversation; we have to infer what is being said at the other end in order to reconstruct the situation for ourselves" (*Answers to Questions* [Grand Rapids: Zondervan Publishing House, 1972], p. 93).

3. The reference in Mark 6:13 is to an earlier restricted mission under Jesus' personal direction.

4. On this perplexing subject A. C. Gaebelein says: "Faith is not blind confidence that demands to get whatever we want, for this in effect, as one has said, would dethrone God, and place the sceptre in our hands, making God merely an obedient and irresisting power to do our unwise bidding. Dr. Brookes in quoting the prayer promises of our Lord in John 14:13, 14 and other passages remarked, 'These are the words of the Lord Jesus Christ Himself, and there is no limitation upon the power they place within the hands of the believer. The only condition is (1) faith and (2) asking in the name of the Son of God, but it will be observed that the condition necessarily implies that the prayer is (3) according to the written Word and (4) the righteous will of God. Without this there might be fanaticism, but there could be no faith. . . . For example, it would not be in keeping with the condition of these blessed promises to pray that we might be rich in this world's possessions, because there is no assurance in the written Word that it is the will of our Father that all His children should be wealthy in gold and silver, in houses and lands, or that it would be best for them to own vast estates. Precisely so, there is no assurance in the written Word that our Father wills all of His children to be exempt from sickness during

this dispensation of suffering, or that it would be best for them to be thus exempt. . . . It is a serious error to insist upon dragging into this age of cross-bearing what will be true only in the bright day of His return' " (*The Healing Question* [New York: Our Hope Publication Office, 1925], pp. 124, 125; numerals mine).

Along this line B. B. Warfield says, "We cannot expect to be emancipated from the laws which govern the action of the forces in the midst of which our life is cast. That would be to take us out of the world. . . . The law of gravity is not suspended in its action on us by our moral character. We cannot grow rich by simply rubbing some Aladdin's lamp and commanding supernatural assistance; economic law will govern the acquisition of wealth in our case as in that of others. . . . The same laws on which you depend for the harvest of corn, you may equally depend on for the harvests of disease which you reap year after year. We live then in a complex of forces out of which we cannot escape, so long as we are in this world, and these forces make for disease and death" (*Counterfeit Miracles* [New York: Charles Scribner's Sons, 1918], pp. 178, 179).

Finally, Sir Robert Anderson has some pertinent words on the subject: ". . . Many . . . are sorely distressed at the seeming failure of the prayer-promises of the Gospels. . . Our Lord impressed on His disciples . . . that they too could command . . . even the moving of a mountain. And He added, 'And all things whatsoever ye shall ask in prayer, believing, ye shall receive ' (Matt. xxi. 20-22). How many there are who in intensest earnestness have claimed such promises, and have reaped bitter disappointment which has staggered their faith!

. . . The Christian should bow in presence of such words, 'according to His will.' . . . The Christian too commonly makes his own longings, or his supposed interests, and not the Divine will, the basis of his prayer; he goes on to persuade himself that his request will be granted; he then regards this 'faith' as a pledge that he has been heard; and finally, when the issue belies his confident hopes, he gives way to bitterness and unbelief. True faith is always prepared for a refusal. Some, we read, 'through faith,' 'obtained promises'; but, no less 'through faith,' 'others were tortured, not accepting deliverance.' . . . It is a solemn thing to make unconditional demands upon God" (*The Silence of God* [Grand Rapids: Kregel Publications, 1952], pp. 204-207).

5

HEALING AND THE ATONEMENT

The idea has been promoted in some quarters that healing is to be found through Christ's atonement, that He suffered to make provision for the bodily needs of His children as well as for their souls' needs. It is said that healing of the body may be claimed by faith in Christ's work just as surely as salvation from sin.

To call this in question would seem to cast doubt upon the completeness of Christ's sacrificial work. Also it would seem to challenge God's love for His children and His willingness to do for them all that might be for their good. Here let us say that no doubts are entertained in regard to either the efficaciousness of Christ's atonement nor God's great love toward His own. That which needs to be looked into is not the fact of these points but their application. The main issue is, What is God's perfect will at any time in regard to His children's temporal welfare and what are the steps in His wide-ranging program for them?

The assertion that healing is in the atonement is sometimes grounded in certain Scripture passages as, ". . . The chastisement of our peace was upon him; and with his stripes we are healed" (Isa. 53:5), or ". . . Himself took our infirmities, and bare our sicknesses" (Matt. 8:17). These have already been examined in chapter 2. To that extent the question before us has already been answered.

Other considerations, however, touch the problem. The

implications of this teaching are larger than might immediately be recognized, and getting the entire picture before us will help toward a right understanding of the subject.

When healing in the atonement is advocated, it is pointed out that Christ's sacrifice was to pay the whole debt of sin, that His redeeming work was to meet fully all that was brought about as a result of the blight of man's transgression. That work, then, was incomplete and inadequate if salvation from bodily afflictions is not part of what He achieved.

To this, two things may be said, and these should largely clear up the matter.

BENEFITS OF THE ATONEMENT—BUT WHEN?

First, Christ, in His substitutionary death, did provide a full redemption. No question here. The only question is, *When* are all the benefits of that great sacrificial work to be realized? It has already been seen that some, yes many, of the fruits of His sacrifice are yet future. That very specifically applies to the body. "Ourselves also, which have the firstfruits of the Spirit, even we ourselves groan within ourselves, waiting for the adoption, to wit, the redemption of our body" (Rom. 8:23). The "waiting" for the body's benefits must be taken into account. Enlarging upon these anticipated blessings is the statement, "The creature itself also shall be delivered from the bondage of corruption into the glorious liberty of the children of God" (Rom. 8:21). Note the future tense used. We look forward to the glorification of our mortal bodies. (See also Philippians 3:20 and 21; 1 John 3:2.)

Our salvation should be recognized as threefold. It embraces spirit, soul and body. It is also progressive. "Each in his own order" (1 Cor. 15:23, ASV). Our spirits *have been* fully saved from eternal doom. Our minds and hearts *are being* saved or sanctified as we daily yield all to God and let His Spirit take full possession. Our bodies *will be* redeemed and glorified in that future day when they are fashioned like unto His glorious body. What a hope! Christ's work is the basis, and personal faith is the means whereby all this is assured to us.

The second thought here is that if the atonement covers our bodily needs now, why should it not similarly include other needs that grew out of the effects of sin, the penalty of which Christ met?

Sin brought forth death. Through the atonement do we escape the cold hand of death? If we can claim by faith complete recovery from bodily ills, why not complete victory now over its counterpart—death? On the contrary, we are distinctly told that death is "the last enemy that shall be destroyed" (1 Cor. 15:26). This statement confirms that while this enemy is included in Christ's work, yet its final achievement is the last to be realized, only at a point in the future.

Sorrow at the loss of loved ones bows down our hearts with grief as we journey through life. Why the pining and weeping if sin's effects have been nullified? In answer, the Word tells us that someday, far out ahead, "there shall be no more death, neither sorrow, nor crying, neither shall there be any more pain: for the former things are passed away" (Rev. 21:4). The hatred, strife and ill-treatment felt by so many children of God at one time or another in this world all result from sin. Sin has been paid for, but we are not yet wholly delivered from these vexations.

Further, toil and sweat, weariness from labor, the aggravating impact of cold, hunger and pain are all parts of what came about through sin's advent into the world. Are they eradicated for the faithful through the atonement? Someday their entire removal will be seen as a result of Christ's perfect work, but no right-thinking person claims full relief from these now. To be sure, Christ's presence and sustaining grace help break the overbearing weight of these things for the Christian; He softens their impact and gives strength to cheerfully carry on. In just the same way He imparts grace and help to the believer in the presence of bodily affliction. For all of this we are grateful to God, realizing that His undergirding is but the foretaste of future blessings, blessings which will far outshine anything we know down here, all purchased for us by the Savior's work.

THE CURSE BORNE AND THE CURSE REMOVED

As proof of the benefits supposed to be presently found in the atonement, the words are sometimes cited, "Christ hath redeemed us from the curse of the law, being made a curse for us "(Gal. 3:13). This would imply that we should be spared all that was a part of the curse of sin on the human race, including bodily ills. Here also two considerations will help.

First, the text, strictly speaking, refers to the "curse of the law," not to the curse immediately growing out of Adam and Eve's transgression. The "curse of the law" was the spiritual condemnation of the law for those who could not keep it (and none could). It cursed us all by showing us our sin, our guilt before God, the exceeding sinfulness of sin. But believers are now redeemed from that judicial condemnation by what Christ endured.

Actually, believers have not yet been delivered from the curse of sin, but from the condemnation of sin. As far as our present state is concerned, Christ's death in our behalf involved sin's penal consequences, not its pathological.

Second, even if the Galatians' passage had reference to the curse connected with the Fall, the question could be asked again, Why not at once claim the removal of every aspect of that curse? Part of that original curse was thorns and thistles in the ground. They are still with us. They are with the godly farmer and the most devout gardener as well as with the unbelieving children of this world. Someday the golden age will break; then the desert will blossom as the rose, and the curse from the ground will be removed. But that day has not dawned yet.

The pain of childbearing is part of the Edenic curse. Do the ones who demand everything in the atonement claim release from that now? If what has been suggested is true, godly women should know deliverance here also, but sadly they do not find it so. Similarly, the enmity between Satan and the woman, as well as that between their seeds, was part of the curse. We see no evidence up to now that all this has been removed.

No, we await the final lifting of the curse. We await the renewal of all nature. The whole creation groans and travails in pain until now (Rom. 8:22). But we have the pledge of a better day to dawn in God's good time. That day, thank God, will bring in the full fruit of Christ's atonement.

One still greater witness remains, found in the last chapter of the Bible where the consummation of all things is reached.

Then and only then is it said, and specifically so: "There shall be no more curse" (Rev. 22:3). No trials and struggles would lead up to this point if the curse had been removed earlier. But then, happily, the last vestige of sin's awful blight will be forever put away.

APOSTOLIC TESTIMONY AND EXPERIENCE

The problem may be looked at in another way. If healing is in the atonement as is the salvation of the soul, a true saint of God should claim all the benefits of the atonement and should not have to endure sickness. Yet this has not been the case.

Examples abound of godly believers who suffer great physical affliction. Some of these are the most devout and consecrated persons who can be found.[1] And the testimony of many, amid their deep suffering, is a wonderful tribute to their faith and confidence in the Savior.

But first observe some Biblical examples. Look at the apostle Paul. He says he was "not a whit behind the very chiefest apostles" (2 Cor. 11:5). He was caught up into paradise, into the third heaven, where he heard things beyond what he was permitted to utter (2 Cor. 12:2, 4). To him were revealed mysteries for which he was dependent on no other man on earth (Gal. 1:12; 2:2; Eph. 3:2, 3). More than once the Lord spoke personally to him from Heaven (Acts 9:4-5; 18:9, 10; 22:17-21; 23:11; 27:23, 24). He was the channel through whom more New Testament epistles were written than all other apostles combined.

However, the apostle Paul was afflicted with bodily sickness. How could that be if healing in the atonement is for believers? Paul speaks of his "infirmity of the flesh" in Galatians 4:13 and 14, and there is no indication that he was in a backslidden state when that came upon him. The same word for "infirmity" is found in John 11:4 where it is rendered "sickness," and in Acts 28:9 as "diseases." In Luke 13:11-13 this term "infirmity" applies to a crippled woman, and in John 5:5 to the bedridden man at the pool of Bethesda. Since in Paul's case the infirmity was said to be "of the flesh," there is no question that it was a physical ailment, although a few have vainly tried to avoid the force of this.[2]

Again, Paul speaks about his "thorn in the flesh" (2 Cor.

12:7). The context indicates that it was something from which Paul suffered intensely. If healing is in the atonement, why did not Paul realize deliverance? Had Paul's faith lapsed, or was he out of the will of God at this time? Just the opposite! It came at the very time when Paul was caught up into Heaven and was given "abundance of revelations" (2 Cor. 12:1-5). That is the very occasion when he should have realized the utmost benefits of the atonement. Yet at the time of his highest exaltation this came upon him. This "messenger of Satan" (2 Cor. 12:7) was apparently deliberately allowed by God for a purpose (in the same way in which Satan was permitted to afflict Job, Job 1).

If atonement was made for the sicknesses of God's children, what right did Paul have to be sick? Did Paul fail to have the faith needed to claim all that he should have? On the contrary, we are told to follow the faith of men like Paul (Heb. 13:7; 1 Thess. 1:6; 2 Thess. 3:7, 9). Paul, commending Timothy, says, "Thou didst follow my . . . faith . . . sufferings . . ." (2 Tim. 3:10, 11, ASV).

This devoted apostle prayed for the removal of his bodily affliction, and his repeated prayer brought him no healing. But God told him it was better for him to go on suffering with it (2 Cor. 12:8-10). He was informed that it was the divine will that he not be cured.

Rather than telling Paul to claim healing, God told Paul that His—God's—strength is made perfect through weakness—Paul's weakness, that is, human weakness (2 Cor. 12:9). Think of it! Instead of weakness and sickness being a reproach upon the child of God (which would be the case if it were now covered by the atonement), it is rather something in which to glory, something through which to honor the Lord. So Paul says, "Most gladly therefore will I rather glory in my infirmities" (v. 9), and, "I take pleasure in infirmities" (v. 10)! Where is the doctrine of healing in the atonement in the light of all of this?

We have already seen how some of the apostle Paul's companions were plagued with bodily ills. We don't know much about the spiritual state of some of these individuals. However, of Epaphroditus we read that he was "sick nigh unto death" (Phil. 2:27). Was Epaphroditus faithless or out of fellowship with the Lord? Quite otherwise, for we read of him, ". . . Hold such in reputation: Because for the work of Christ he was nigh unto death, not regarding his life" (vv. 29, 30). His sacrificial commitment to Christ was a model to be held up. His condition is not said to be because he had sinned or had failed to claim what was rightly his. After some time he recovered because "God had mercy on him" (v. 27). That is the true ground for healing. It is mercy, not something ours by right or to be had on demand, but only as and when it pleases God to grant it.

Or take the case of Timothy. He was very dear to Paul; but more, he was highly esteemed and commended to the churches. Paul would hardly have spoken so favorably of him if he had been deficient in faith or failed to claim all that was available to a true child of God. The record of him is very revealing. In 1 Timothy 5:23 Paul says to him, "Drink no longer water, but use a little wine for thy stomach's sake and thine often infirmities." Two things of significance are seen here.

First, Timothy suffered from debilitating stomach trouble. Furthermore, we are distinctly told that he even had "often infirmities," or, as most modern translators have it, "frequent" attacks, ailments or illnesses,[3] or "recurring illness."[4] How could one be so used of the Lord if he failed to see and appropriate the full blessings of the work of Christ?

Second, the apostle tells Timothy to take something for his malady. We see here the negative and the positive. Negatively, Timothy is not told to apply to his sickness the work of Christ. Positively, he is to take a readily accessible product for his affliction, an earthly means for the body's benefit.

This is the Timothy of whom, in this same first epistle of Paul to him, it is said, ". . . A good minister of Jesus Christ, nourished up in the words of faith and of good doctrine, whereunto thou hast attained" (4:6); and, ". . . Thou . . . hast professed a good profession before many witnesses" (6:12). No rebuke here for failure, no suggestion of entering more completely into the full sphere of Christ's atonement.

One advocate of the healing doctrine advanced in all seriousness a most ingenious explanation of Paul's advice to Timothy. He concludes (we know not on what basis) that in the community where Timothy lived the water was bad, so impure in fact, that the apostle had to direct him to use wine (fermented) as a substitute!

I lived at one time in a village in the Philippines where the water was so contaminated that it was unsafe for domestic use. If I had followed the advice above, I would have drawn no converts to the Lord; in fact, I would have been invited, if not assisted to leave town, for surely I soon would have been unable to walk a straight line through the village![5]

From the Scriptures examined, we conclude that there is no clear Bible warrant for assuming that the people of God are expected in this life to find, through the atonement, full deliverance from sickness, pain or death.

ATONEMENT, SICKNESS AND FAITH

Extravagant claims have been made by advocates of healing who hold that healing is in the atonement as surely as salvation. Lack of faith, they say, holds back the full blessings from us.

How unlike the soul-saving aspect of Christ's work this presumed healing teaching is. In healing meetings many people have gone forward to claim by faith the healing of the body, yet have not secured it, while some who have claimed to have found it have lost it and fallen back into the same or a worse physical condition. But when, for the soul's needs, one lays hold by faith on Christ's atonement, he immediately receives salvation, his sins are forgiven, and he is born again. One can rejoice that there is no failure here.

On the other side of the picture, some who do not believe that healing is presently in the atonement have prayed simple prayers for physical relief and have found it, believing that God met their need through humble but earnest prayer alone.

The philosophy of healing in the atonement cuts deep. The logic of it would be that since Christ died to give us physical health as well as spiritual benefits, a child of God putting true faith in the Savior should receive as sure deliverance from sickness as he receives complete forgiveness of sins. Both sickness and the soul's alienation from God being results of sin, both should alike be removed by a similar exercise of faith. Yet recovery from physical ills by such singular faith has not been observed under the worldwide preaching of the gospel. If it had been, what a demonstration the Christian community would have left before a skeptical world!

Much is at stake. If a believer asks for healing and is not healed, how does he know that when he asked for forgiveness, his sins were forgiven? The believer should have a right to expect the reception of each just as surely and on the same basis. We read that there is no condemnation to them that are in Christ Jesus. Can it be said similarly that there is no sickness to them that are in Christ Jesus?

When a man sins he is personally guilty before God, but no such thing is necessarily concluded regarding sickness. Judicially speaking it is sin, not disease, that needs atonement. Since Christ bore our sins, we are not to bear the penalty of them. If Christ to the same extent bore our sicknesses, no believer should bear the pain of them. The presence of sickness would argue the absence of faith which unites one to Christ. (Thousands of consecrated missionaries have paid a great toll in sickness in pestilent lands. They must have been devoid of even the faith which ordinary believers should possess!)

Healing for the body, it must be admitted, is not found in the atonement the same as the salvation of the soul. There is no indication in Scripture that such benefit is to be realized in our present state.

NOTES:

1. George Muller of the faith orphanages in England, perhaps the greatest exemplar in modern times of a life of prayer and superabounding faith, was himself often sick, even being laid aside for extended periods because of physical suffering. And his best-known biographer, Arthur T. Pierson, records how, just after Mrs. Muller's father died, both of their own little children "were very ill," culminating in their only son being taken. Both parents "were divinely upheld. They had felt no liberty in prayer for the child's recovery, dear as he was." (*George Muller of Bristol* [New York: Loizeaux Brothers, 1944], p. 120).

2. Since Paul's infirmity was "of the flesh," note that the word *flesh* is used in sharp contrast with the word *spirit*. (Examples are seen in Matthew 26:41; Luke 24:39; John 3:6; 6:63; Romans 2:28, 29; 8:4, 5; 1

Corinthians 5:5; Galatians 3:3; 4:29; 5:16, 17; 6:8; Ephesians 6:12; Philippians 3:3.) Flesh is also contrasted with the "mind" (Rom. 7:25), and with "conscience" (1 Pet. 3:21). Reference is made to "our mortal flesh" (2 Cor. 4:11). All of this leaves no question that the apostle suffered in the *flesh*.

3. As found in the New International Version, New American Standard, New Scofield Bible, Williams, Amplified, Weymouth, and others.

4. Berkeley Version.

5. What *did* I do? Boil the water, of course. Wherever food can be cooked, water can be boiled, assuring its safety.

6

The Purpose of Miraculous Healing

The question most naturally arises, Why were miracles commonly manifest in certain periods and not at other times? To be more specific, if healings were so prevalent in New Testament days, why should they not be so now? Physical suffering is just as burdensome today as it ever was; the afflicted long just as earnestly for relief. Is our God less concerned with His children's welfare today than formerly?

The answer in simple terms is that miracles (such as healings) were given for a definite purpose. When that purpose was fulfilled, the necessity for them no longer existed. To understand this it is well to review God's ways of working in history.

It should be noted that crucial turning points in God's dealing with men were often introduced by miracles. But either suddenly—or more commonly gradually—they ceased to be manifest. There were long and perplexing periods when the people of God found themselves in various needs, but no miracles were forthcoming.

The periods of Abraham, Isaac and Jacob were marked by the absence of special miracles, although God dealt with His people in remarkable ways, as always.

Probably the most distinctive turning point in Old Testament times was the introduction of the Mosaic era. The miracles at the hands of Moses and Aaron need no amplification. After the conquest of Canaan and into the times of the judges these wonders faded as the commonly expected thing. In fact poor, distraught Gideon plaintively cries, "If the LORD be with us, why then is all this befallen us? and where be all his miracles which our fathers told us of?" (Judg. 6:13). People today are asking the same question and are no less confounded than was Gideon. What might be termed miracles possibly occur on rare occasions, but they are not the order of the day.

From Samuel through the extended period of the United Kingdom (closing with Solomon), miracles appear to have been largely absent. A new and vexatious era (the division of the kingdom and oppression by surrounding nations) was introduced during the time of the prophets Elijah and Elisha when miracles reappeared, but the days of these two prophets were relatively short. The rest of the long period to the close of the Old Testament was virtually free of miracles—at least common miracles of healing.

The same observation carries over into the New Testament period. The New Testament opens with a prominent resurgence of miracles; most appropriately so. Deity in Person interposed upon the pages of human history. The long-promised Redeemer, the Desire of all nations, at last made His momentous appearance. Miracles quite naturally found a place.

Messiah's departure from earth's scenes did not mean a resumption here below of the former somewhat static order of events. Something new was introduced into the march of history. A new institution—the Church—was to challenge Rome's dominant influence. And the advent of that life-transforming movement was likewise to be accompanied by signs and wonders, without which its appearance would scarcely have been noticed. But once its impact was felt and its future assured, the miracles were no longer essential to its continued welfare.

Miracles, then, serve the purpose, when God so directs, of arresting widespread attention and attesting a new order; but when their purpose is fulfilled, God in His sovereignty seems pleased to withdraw such miracle-working.

REASONS FOR CHANGING WAYS

The principle just enunciated has been widely recognized by prominent students of God's ways with men.

George Park Fisher, well-known writer on church history and other themes, speaking of revelation in the broad sense of God manifesting Himself, says,

> The Gospel miracles are for the express purpose of attesting revelation. They are the proper counterpart and proof of revelation. They occur, with few exceptions, only at the marked epochs of revelation,—the Mosaic era, the reform and advance of the Old Testament religion under the great prophets, and in connection with the ministry of Christ and the founding of the church. . . .
>
> When they have once taken place . . . there is no call for a perpetual interruption of the course of nature.[1]

On this a British scholar quotes Dr. George Macdonald:

> The Scriptures record three eras signalized by displays of the supernatural, which three periods stand associated with Moses, Elijah, and the Lord Jesus Christ. . . . Only these deserve to be called the ages of miracles. The reasons for the distinction must be sought in peculiarity of circumstances, and in special Providential ends requiring extraordinary measures for their accomplishment. . . . These were crises of unparalleled importance. If it ever comported with the wisdom and goodness of the Supreme, for His power to be exceptionally seen on the theatre of human affairs, it would be fitting for the manifestation to appear at such times. . . . Every one of the three *clusters of signs* stands when and where it was most to be expected.[2]

Dr. William E. Biederwolf said:

> Miracles were not continuous throughout the period. Abraham, David, Daniel, and other mighty men of faith did no miracles. Miracles were manifested only on a very few special occasions when some great crisis was upon the people of God. . . .
>
> All of God's *beginnings* as touching creation are wonderful. It it to be expected that it would be even so with the beginning of the spiritual creation—the Christian Church.[3,4]

How may all of this be applied when we come down more specifically to the days of the New Testament apostles, the times from which we might be expected, if at all, to take our cue? An answer is not lacking.

In their long standard work on the apostle Paul, Conybeare and Howson say:

> We are not to suppose that the Apostles were always able to work miracles at will. An influx of supernatural power was given to them, at the time, and according to the circumstances that required it. And the character of the miracles was not always the same. They were accommodated to the peculiar forms of sin, superstition, and ignorance they were required to oppose.[5]

B. B. Warfield is perhaps more direct. Speaking of the unusual gifts of that day, he says:

> The immediate end for which they were given is . . . the authentication of the Apostles as messengers from God. . . . The charismata belonged, in a true sense, to the Apostles, and constituted one of the signs of an Apostle. [They were] to authenticate the Apostles as the authoritative founders of the church. . . . The extraordinary gifts belong to the extraordinary office and showed themselves only in connection with its activities.[6]

The well-known Lange's Commentary, in the volume on Paul's last epistle, 2 Timothy, quotes from Starke: "Miracles were used only as introductory to the preaching of the gospel, and as confirmatory of it."[7]

A. C. Gaebelein comes to the conclusion:

> The miracles of healing, as well as others, were essential in the beginning of the new dispensation, and equally essential for the introduction of Christianity among the Gentiles. . . . These sign gifts were for the beginning of the Church, but are not needed for the completion of the Church, nor for the edification of that Body. When God revealed all He meant to reveal, sight and signs end and "we walk by faith and not by sight."[8]

These excerpts speak for themselves and demonstrate the widely recognized principle that miracles have well-defined limits.

THE SCRIPTURAL PRINCIPLE

What are the indications in Scripture that these healing gifts would not be characteristic of the entire Church Age?

In Hebrews we read of the great salvation "which at the first began to be spoken by the Lord, and was confirmed unto us by them that heard him; God also bearing them witness, both with signs and wonders, and with divers miracles. . ." (Heb. 2:3, 4). Note the "at the first." This is in perfect accord with the principle just reviewed. The establishment of a new economy introduced by great miracles is readily understood.

Human nature is slow to accept change. Most markedly is this so when people's relationships are changed, when accustomed usages are disrupted, when long accepted socio-economic-political norms are forced into dissolution.

Historians covering the period before us have remarked how deeply the Romans generally looked down upon the Jews; and as to the Palestinian Jews resenting Rome, there is no need to elaborate.

Now abruptly something comes upon the scene which would change things. It would radically disrupt the entire status quo. Nothing is impossible with God, but to introduce an earth-shaking change, miracles are more to be expected than not.

The Jewish people have long been recognized as rather clannish, tending to be unyielding to things outside their own cherished institutions. Their difference with others is indicated in the words written to the Corinthians, "For the Jews require a sign [the same word as *miracle*], and the Greeks seek after wisdom" (1 Cor. 1:22). It is no wonder, then, that signs or miracles should accompany an entirely new order of things that would so largely involve the Jews. The miracle signs should have helped convince them of the truth of the new message and of the divine purpose in the new institution, the Church (cf. 1 Cor. 14:21).

BABYHOOD AND MATURITY

Paul chided the Corinthians because they did not want to stand on the newer, higher level. He says he writes to them "even as unto babes in Christ" (1 Cor. 3:1), and he appeals to them to leave behind the babyhood that requires something spectacular (1 Cor. 14:20).

Early in Paul's ministry miracles played a role. But as the gospel became established in the Roman world, miracles—particularly miracles of healing—faded out. Paul left a companion behind because of illness (2 Tim. 4:20); he advised another to take something for his infirmities (1 Tim. 5:23); and he commended—rather than censured—a fellow worker who was critically ill (Phil. 2:26, 27). Paul himself endured deep physical suffering (2 Cor. 12:7-10). The Jews had been given all necessary witness, and the gospel had now been effectively introduced among the Gentiles.

The Corinthian portion of Scripture dealing with sign gifts, including healing, says definitely that when that which is perfect—complete, mature—is come, that which is in part—incomplete, imperfect—shall be done away (1 Cor. 13:10), adding, "But when I became a man, I put away childish things" (v. 11). Have we today become men? With the help of God may we attain that level. (Cf. 1 Corinthians 3:1; 13:11; 14:20; Galatians 4:3, 19; Ephesians 4:14; Hebrews 5:12, 13.)

This encouragement to higher things is seen still further when 1 Corinthians 12 to 14 is considered as a whole. These three chapters are recognized as a unit, the passage having to do with spiritual gifts. Healing is mentioned in chapter 12 as one of the gifts (vv. 9, 28). Chapter 13 brings to the fore something that is superior to gifts, something more to be desired, and indeed something more enduring—love.

Chapter 13 makes passing mention of certain gifts, but healing is not referred to. Chapter 14 discusses even more the limited exercise of gifts, but healing is not alluded to, apparently anticipating its having served its purpose. Those things which have fulfilled their mission should be recognized for what they were and no longer be sought in view of that which supersedes them.

THE CESSATION OF MIRACLES

Some scholarly witness has already been seen on the matter of miracles serving a special purpose. With the fulfillment of that purpose, miracles are no longer needed. Let us observe what has been said particularly on why we today may not expect miraculous healings as a regular experience.

Handley C. G. Moule points up reasons why these miracles were peculiar to the early period of the church:

> I do gather, both from the history of the Church and from that pregnant Scripture, I Corinthians 13:8, that *on the whole* the commonly called miraculous displays of that power were intended for the first days only, or at least in a degree altogether peculiar. That period had characteristic conditions and needs

which can never quite recur, even where the Gospel is a new thing among the heathen of our time. For the Gospel was then everywhere and absolutely new, with no history as yet behind it, no results of long years to give it their credentials. I do not think, with some earnest Christians, that the Christian Church is "responsible" for the abeyance of miraculous manifestation, by a lack of faith while faith might at any time claim the wonder-working power. I believe on the other hand that subtile dangers and strong temptations lie concealed where the Christian, or the community, is eager for the gift of such miraculous faculties rather than for an ever-deepening abasement of self before the Holy One and an ever closer and more chastened walk with Him. . . . It seems to me to be certain not merely that *upon the whole* such operation is not the will of God now as it was of old, but that this is so because more and more His people are to be led in His plan of teaching to rest in that "more excellent way" which already in that wonderful first age the Apostle preferred to even "the best gifts" of other kind (I Corinthians 12:31).[9]

Rackham's scholarly commentary on the Acts takes up the matter of these declining miracles in the developing church.

At the beginning these phenomena formed a regular and unfailing mark of church life: and their freshness and abundance made a deeper impression than now. . . . If such unique miracles ceased to appear in the church, it is not hard to assign a reason. Later on the effect was produced in other ways. The spread of Christianity made faith as it were at home in the world; it restored it to its place as a natural faculty which did not need an abnormal event to give it birth. The environment, i.e. the mind of the world, has also changed. An abnormal event today would not arouse real faith. It would either be denied, or, if believed, it would probably only minister to curiosity and superstition.[10]

Two other authorities may be quoted, not so much on the matter of miracle works fulfilling a peculiar purpose (as seen before), but upon the matter of these signs ceasing as a needed witness in the ongoing Church.

R. C. Trench on the miracles says:

It is not my belief that she [the post-apostolic Church] has this gift of working miracles, nor yet that she was intended to have it. . . . The Church of Christ, with its immense and evident superiorities of all kinds over everything with which it is brought in contact, and some portions of which superiority every man must recognize, is itself now the great witness and proof of the truth which it delivers. The truth, therefore, has no longer need to vindicate itself by appeal to something else.[11]

Again, B. B. Warfield says:

Miracles do not appear on the page of Scripture vagrantly, here, there, and elsewhere indifferently, without . . . reason. . . . Their abundant display in the Apostolic Church is the mark of the richness of the Apostolic age in revelation; and when this revelation period closed, the period of miracle-working had passed by also, as a mere matter of course. . . .

Therefore it is that the miraculous working which is but the sign of God's revealing power, cannot be expected to continue, and in point of fact does not continue, after the revelation of which it is the accompaniment has been completed. . . . By as much as the one gospel suffices for all lands and all peoples and all times, by so much does the miraculous attestation of that one single gospel suffice for all lands and all times, and no further miracles are to be expected in connection with it.[12]

All that has been pointed out does not mean that God has, since the cessation of special miraculous healing, simply abandoned His children to suffering with no regard to relief. By no means. Our Lord is still "touched with the feeling of our infirmities." Two main avenues of help are yet open to the afflicted since the disappearance of extraordinary healing ministries.

First, the avenue of prayer remains open. No limitations are laid down in respect thereto. God still hears and answers in remarkable ways. Second, in the providence of God medical science has advanced apace. Both natural remedies and the skill of physicians are available to the suffering, though within understandable limitations.

But the purpose behind the bestowing of special gifts at the commencement of this age has become clear; that purpose having been fulfilled, we should be satisfied to leave the rest in the hands of God. Now after nineteen centuries of witness to attest the gospel, we should be able to stand without the sensational or spectacular to sustain our commitment to the truth of God.

As Dr. Hagen, a medical missionary to India so well says:

Why, then, does not God perform many more miracles of healing than he does? It seems clear to me that as a regular thing God does not want to produce supernatural miracles of healing and that this is the reason we seldom see any repetitions of the miracles of the New Testament. An out-and-out miracle of healing is, I believe, in God's eyes an inferior method of handling human disease. It is a concession to a generation that is always demanding signs and wonders (John 4:48). If God were to go beyond the laws of nature and produce miracles of healing as a sort of everyday matter here and there throughout the world, we would run into serious difficulties.

Cures wrought easily through an act of simple, childlike faith would undermine the whole system of natural law and order. They would make people disinclined to learn or study that law and order. The world would become a hotbed of spiritual, political favoritism. . . . It would be arrogant of me as a human being to assume that I am so important to God's plan that he must transcend the laws of nature to heal me from my disease now. God may well find it much better for me to endure the disease I have, to cope with it as best I can, to carry it bravely, even to surmount the handicap it brings.[13, 14]

NOTES:

1. George Park Fisher, *The Grounds of Theistic and Christian Belief* (London: Hodder & Stoughton, 1908), pp. 281, 282.

2. Quoted by Robert Tuck, *A Handbook of Biblical Difficulties* (New York: Thomas Whittaker, 1888), pp. 509, 510.

3. William E. Biederwolf, *Whipping-Post Theology* (Grand Rapids: William B. Eerdmans, 1934), p. 123.

4. Equally to the point are the words of Richard C. Trench, long recognized as an outstanding authority on the miracles, when he presents this analysis: "The powers evermore at work for the upholding of the natural world would have been manifestly insufficient for its first creation; there were others which must have presided at its birth, but which now, having done their work, have fallen back, and left it to follow the laws of its ordinary development. It is only according to the analogies of that which thus everywhere surrounds us, to presume that it was even so with the beginnings of the spiritual creation—the Christian Church. . . . Shall we count it strange, then, that the coming in of a new order . . . into the entire world, should have been wonderful? It would have been inexplicable if it had been otherwise. . . . 'Miracles,'

says Fuller, 'are the swaddling clothes of the infant Churches'; and, we may add, not the garments of the full grown. They were the proclamation that the king was mounting his throne; who, however, is not proclaimed every day, but only on his accession" (*Notes on the Miracles of our Lord* [Grand Rapids: Baker Book House, 1968], pp. 31, 32).

5. W. J. Conybeare and J. S. Howson, *The Life and Epistles of St. Paul* (New York: Charles Scribner & Co., 1869), vol. 2, p. 22.

6. Warfield, *Counterfeit Miracles*, pp. 21, 23.

7. J. P. Lange, *Commentary on the Holy Scriptures: II Timothy* (Grand Rapids: Zondervan Publishing House, n.d.), p. 119.

8. Gaebelein, *The Healing Question*, pp. 33, 43.

9. Handley C. G. Moule, *Veni Creator* (London: Pickering and Inglis, n.d.), pp. 214, 215.

10. Richard B. Rackham, *The Acts of the Apostles* (London: Methuen & Co., 1953), pp. 223-225.

11. Trench, *Notes on the Miracles of Our Lord*, pp. 30, 31.

12. Warfield, *Counterfeit Miracles*, pp. 25-27.

13. Kristofer Hagen, *Faith and Health* (Philadelphia: Muhlenberg Press, 1961), pp. 60, 61.

14. Two further testimonies of prominent students bear out what has gone before. Being rather lengthy their words have been reserved for inclusion here.

A scholarly and widely read writer of a few years ago, Professor A. B. Bruce, sees the distinction between the spiritual and the physical as a leading reason why material good should not be elevated to the level of the soul's benefits. He says: "Was it Christ's purpose that it [redemption] should assume this dual form in parallel streams of spiritual and corporeal blessing running as rivers of life throughout all the Christian ages? . . . The cure of disease, though very prominent in our Lord's public ministry, was not co-ordinate with, but subordinate to, His work as Saviour from sin, and it served once for all certain purposes in connection with the Christian revelation. . . . But it may be asked, why should the manifestation of Christ's sympathy with human suffering be a mere fact of past history, why should it not go on now as of old in the same benignant way, resulting in extensive, signal, supernatural healing of disease in answer to the prayer of faith? Why should not a healing ministry of the exalted Christ form an integral, perpetual part of the work of the kingdom? Would it not . . . worthily exhibit Christianity to the world as having for its twofold aim the extinction at once of disease and of sin? . . .

"Apparently the explanation is this, that it has been generally felt that disease is not on the same level with sin; that physical evil in general, of which bodily disease is only one form, cannot be co-ordinated with moral evil as of equal importance, and that while the divine plan of redemption contemplates complete deliverance from all evil, each part comes in its own order, spiritual deliverance first as most urgent and important, physical deliverance in the end, coming at last after long waiting in answer to the longing of the whole creation. . . .

"The question is, Ought the Church to put the healing of disease on the same doctrinal foundation as the pardon of sin, and to announce it systematically as an esential part of the Gospel? . . . This theory unduly magnifies the benefit of merely physical health. . . . The exegetical basis of the theory is very slender. . . . The two interests—the lower interest of the body and the higher interest of the spirit—are not completely compatible in this present state of things. . . . The treasure is in an earthen vessel. The outward man perishes, not only while, but because the inward man is renewed day by day" (*The Miraculous Element in the Gospels* [London: Hodder & Stoughton, 1902], pp. 315, 316, 318, 319).

Another British student of this broad area of interest, W. Graham Scroggie, in writing chiefly on the matter of speaking in tongues, includes all such wonders of the apostolic days when he says: "I do not hesitate to say that this sign was never intended to be permanent. . . . Signs of this kind are no more a part of the Christian witness, than the Mosaic ritual is the form of Christian worship. . . . The period . . . is in each instance a transition period, with its peculiar characteristics. . . . Let us remember that at the time of which we are speaking there was no New Testament to which appeal could be made, and for this reason, in part, no doubt, signs were vouchsafed to them as evidence of the Divine presence and power. But now, the New Testament . . . is our power and our authority, rendering the working of miracles unnecessary. If it be claimed that we may now do all that the apostles did, how is it that no one is writing Holy Scripture? . . . The present is not an age of sensuous signs, but of spiritual power, and if, for lack of experience of that power, we resort to what is sensuous, we need not be surprised that the devil makes the most of the opportunity. . . .

"We conclude, therefore, that the miracles of the apostolic age, which served during that period as signs, have ceased to be displayed, the need for them having been superseded; and that in the present age sensuous evidences have given place to spiritual evidences" (*Speaking with Tongues* [New York: The Book Stall, 1919], pp. 20, 21, 22, 24).

7

UNDERSTANDING PRESENT-DAY HEALINGS

Some people today claim to have been miraculously healed. It is acknowledged that remarkable recoveries have occurred, and these appear to stand as evidence of divine healing in our day. Some who were definitely sick or crippled have become well, both their previous condition and their later improved state being known to friends or loved ones.

We do not desire to evade the impact of these cases—incidents in which something beyond the ordinary course of events seems to have transpired. But people may still wonder as to the actual source or underlying cause of these apparent healings.

SEVERAL POSSIBILITIES

Several possible explanations for what has occurred may be suggested. Some recoveries could even be attributed to a combination of more than one element. Parties involved are often sincere and nothing depreciative is necessarily attributable to them.

The first explanation to be considered is the fact that God does answer prayer. Those dealt with by a prominent divine healing personage before a great throng, as well as those privately anointed or otherwise ministered to, have often been long prayed for; and some are in earnest prayer for themselves. God in His mercy may then be pleased to give the answer—not because of any high state of expectancy or because of any dynamic personality, but because He honors the faithful prayers of His children when and as it might be in accord with His sovereign will.

A second explanation of benefits at times occurring would be the great psychological boost given to some who had real ills, but ills grounded in psychosomatic causes. In an atmosphere of high anticipation where intense feelings are aroused, there is a surge of mental and emotional uplift which actually affects the physical. This is just what was needed. This is recognized even by the medical profession.

A third factor to be considered would be that some who have had real injuries or organic disturbances were already beginning to recover through natural curative processes which normally work in the body. Without any special ministration the healing would have come by itself sooner or later.

A fourth and very definite possibility is that those with imaginary ailments are being helped and believe that they are healed. Indeed, both those with real and those with supposed afflictions may really think—but it is only a matter of their thinking—that they are cured.

Fifth, in recent days more recognition is being given to hypnosis. Its scientific basis is acknowledged. It is used in experimental and investigative fields, and certain ones are applying it in regular practice. Some who have not entered into a technical study of it may have a natural bent toward it or may have acquired a felicitous use of some of its principles and, knowingly or unknowingly, apply it in the area before us. We believe this is a dangerous field even though definite results doubtless have been achieved through its use.

A sixth factor is that still others with ills believe it is a mark of faith to claim healing. They may assume that if they say, "Yes, I believe God is healing me," that God will honor that expression of faith and that the healing will come. On this ground they put forth a little extra effort. Then they have the satisfaction that they have left nothing undone on their part, and withal they feel better.

Seventh, many Bible students and close observers do not discount the possibility of Satanic deception. The heathen magicians of Egypt duplicated certain miracles of Moses and Aaron (Exod. 7 and 8). Jesus warned of demonstrations intended to deceive even the very elect (Matt. 7:22, 23; 24:24). At the end time the man of sin will perform wonders in the sight of the people (2 Thess. 2:8, 9; Rev. 13:12-15). The question may arise, Why would Satan work to benefit people? Remember that Satan can perform apparent good (2 Cor. 11:14, 15) to deceive, and to bring confusion, division and a turning aside among the people of God. It behooves us to be wary of the evil one's devices, to search the Scripture diligently, and to be submissive under the hand of God rather than seeking always our own comfort and well-being.

There is an eighth possibility—though some would hesitate even to hint at it: outright fraud. But this has not been unknown in the history of spectacular healings.

These and other suggestions have not been wanting. Books and papers have been printed containing rather sensational accounts of healings. Radio and television programs have featured testimonials of people cured of the most dire ills. All this sounds very convincing. In fact much of it appears almost too professional. Even where it is claimed a presentation is unrehearsed, the featured personality seems so poised, precise and self-assured that one may wonder if something more does not lie behind the whole thing than appears on the surface. Proposals have not been lacking that some healings could well be staged, testimonials surreptitiously induced, or something of advantage extended to the one being exhibited. It could also be that individuals are made to feel that in professing a miracle, a miracle is more likely to become a reality. Others might be convinced that at any rate their effort is helping a good cause.

Many possibilities thus present themselves. No attempt is made here to give a final answer. All possibilities should be taken into consideration, and one may draw his own conclusions.

RECOGNITION OF ELEMENTS INVOLVED

A number who are interested in this subject have studied certain aspects of these wonder cures. Their observations are worth noting.

Sir Robert Anderson, for many years head of London's famed Scotland Yard (where keen perception was necessarily a top priority), was an acute student of religious interests. His conclusions regarding the claims of miraculous healing are to the point:

Religious miracles claim a passing notice. I do not allude to tricks of priests, but to cases of extraordinary cures from serious illness; and some at least of these appear to be supported by evidence sufficient to establish their truth. The phenomena of hysteria and mimetic disease will probably account for the majority of cases of the kind. Others again may be explained as instances of the power of the mind and will over the body. . . . The progress of disease may be controlled, and even checked, by some mastering influence or emotion which turns the patient's thoughts back to life, and makes him believe he is convalescent. But while the vast majority of seemingly miraculous cures may thus be explained on natural principles, there may perhaps be some which are genuine miracles. There are no limits to the possibilities of faith, and God may thus declare Himself at times. . . .

. . . Among Christians it is pestilently evil to make the exceptional experience of some the rule of faith for all. The Word of God is our guide, and not the experience of fellow-Christians; and when this is ignored the practical consequences are disastrous. The annals of 'faith healing,' as it is called, are rich in cases of mimetic or hysterical disease, but about the spiritual wreckage due to failures innumerable they are silent.[1]

Later, on this side of the Atlantic, L. S. Reed wrote in *The Healing Cults:*

To many it may seem incongruous and unseemly to discuss healing by magic along with healing through religious faith, yet both are essentially the same phenomenon; in both cases the cures, and undoubtedly there are some, are wrought through faith.

[Then he quotes from an article in the *Journal of the American Medical Association*]: "Each system in some way introduces the idea of cure or health after preparing the mind through one means or another to accept it, and the fundamental principle of each system is the assumption that any idea possessing the mind tends to materialize in the body. . . . While the members of these healing cults volubly deny that their work in any way involves hypnotism, they could not fail to note the resemblance were they aware of the facts in the case. Few recognize that there are all stages of subjectivity in hypnotism. . . . The patient by exercising his morale may so completely control his attention that instead of fixating it on his symptoms, though they are of the most distressing nature, he believes himself cured and becomes entirely unaware of the fact that his physical condition remains the same and that his disease is running the natural course of its development."

. . . In religious healing, particularly where states of religious exaltation are invoked, it must be evident that the suggestion of health or cure is linked with and made dynamic by a complex of ideas and emotions of tremendous power.[2]

Seeking to analyze the situation, W. E. Biederwolf wrote:

We find evidence enough of the power of mind over our bodily states, but what the most of us do not appreciate is *the extent to which our entire physiological condition is but the outward expression of our mental attitude.* . . .

We encounter that mental force known as "Suggestion." Suggestion is either Internal or External. As the former it is known as Auto-suggestion, or suggestion made by oneself; while the latter may very properly be called Hetero-suggestion, or suggestion made by another. . . .

We have also what is known as Hypnotic-suggestion. This is, however, but another phase of Hetero-suggestion and finds its sphere of operation in the region of the subconscious mind.

Hypnotism and Telepathy are recognized facts in the scientific world today. And what do we mean by these terms? Simply this: the passive submission to the control of another intelligence and the subsequent transference of thought by this intelligence to the subconscious mind of the first party. . . .

. . . If this imaginative attitude of the mind may become creative of firm and earnest belief that brings with it the calmness and confidence which leads on to that radiant expectancy of which we spoke . . . it is not difficult to conceive of the beneficial physiological effect which . . . will always follow; for with the departure of the disturbing and disquieting elements of fear and foreboding, and with the consequent quiet and normal operation of the vital processes resumed it is conceivable how the *Vis Mediatrix Naturae* (the curative power of nature), which constantly tends toward health, may work toward that end unhindered and undisturbed and thus bring about the patient's recovery.

... With evidence almost inexhaustible, the honest-thinking individual will not fail to see how large a place the mind holds in the healing of the body, both in functional and organic diseases.

History is full of such evidence and all the best medical authority has come to recognize it. Psychotherapy is a word which has come to demand our serious attention. ... The *vast majority* of so-called divine healing and faith healing cases *are simply and solely metaphysical.* [3]

Another who gave extensive study to the subject was Wade H. Boggs. He points out:

It is extremely easy for a layman to be misled regarding the exact nature of a disease. No layman is qualified either to diagnose his own sickness or to determine whether he is completely healed. Public testimonials of healings at moments of great excitement and emotional stress are worthless. For that matter, even doctors with all their scientific means of diagnosis are occasionally deceived. ...

Some ... believe the cures are "psychosomatic." This is a term which is enjoying immense and growing prestige in medical circles. ... It conveys the idea that many diseases, previously thought to be purely physical or chemical, are closely connected with, if not caused by, mental conditions. Thus the methods of faith healers might conceivably be instrumental in curing diseases that have been caused by mental or spiritual conditions. ...

Scientific progress already made in the field of psychosomatic medicine has resulted in tracing a number of specific connections between mental causes and bodily diseases. Other connections are suspected. Nearly all doctors today will readily concede that a wide variety of physical ills have their roots in mental trouble, and that such diseases have often been healed, or have noticeably improved, following the clearing up of a mental disturbance. But ... the exact limits of the mind's influence upon the body have not yet been fixed. [4]

A more recent study of a highly scientific nature has been made by a professor in Harvard Medical School. In *Persuasion and Healing: A Comparative Study of Psychotherapy*, Jerome D. Frank says:

Inexplicable cures of serious organic disease occur in everyday medical practice. Every physician has either personally treated or heard about patients who mysteriously recovered from a seemingly fatal illness. One surgeon has recently assembled from the literature ninety cases of unquestionable cancer that disappeared without adequate treatment. Had these cures occurred after a visit to Lourdes, many would have regarded them as miraculous. . . .

The core of the effectiveness of methods of religious and magical healing seems to lie in their ability to arouse hope by capitalizing on the patient's dependency on others. This dependency ordinarily focuses on one person, the healer, who may work privately with the patient or in a group setting. In either case, the patient's expectation of help is aroused. . . .

From the standpoint of psychotherapy, religious healing, revivalism, and thought reform all highlight the importance of emotions in facilitating or producing attitude change and in affecting one's state of health.[5]

Showing how an emotional buildup or the excitement of the occasion may give a person the boost needed to make operative again functions which apparently were dormant or thought through injury or disease to be beyond the power of functioning, W. E. Biederwolf tells of an actual case in connection with Mrs. Biederwolf's confinement.

The wife of the author was in the Martinsville, Indiana, Sanatorium, and in the same Sanatorium was a woman who was seemingly utterly helpless in her lower limbs. She had to be wheeled about in a chair. They wheeled her to her meals and they wheeled her out for air. They wheeled her to her bath and they wheeled her to her bed. They wheeled her here and they wheeled her there, and they wheeled her everywhere. The Sanatorium caught fire and burned nearly to the ground. As the author's wife threw open her door, the first person she saw was this same woman rushing down the hall, her back loaded with a huge bundle of her belongings. Something had happened to her hitherto helpless (?) limbs.[6]

NOTES:

1. Anderson, *The Silence of God*, pp. 170, 171.

2. Louis S. Reed, *The Healing Cults* (Chicago: The University of Chicago Press, 1932), pp. 100, 102, 103, 104.

3. Biederwolf, *Whipping-Post Theology*, pp. 145, 147, 148, 151, 152, 153.

4. Wade H. Boggs, *Faith Healing and the Christian Faith* (Richmond: John Knox Press, 1956), pp. 22, 24, 25.

5. Jerome D. Frank, *Persuasion and Healing: A Comparative Study of Psychotherapy* (Baltimore: The Johns Hopkins Press, 1961), pp. 57, 62, 96.

6. Biederwolf, *Whipping-Post Theology*, p. 145.

8

SUMMARY

THE DATA SIFTED

Appeal is often made to the example of Christ and the apostles in their healing of the sick. Since they are held up as the ideal of what should be expected, it is well to observe briefly some features of their healings. The most casual examination will reveal that they set a standard far beyond anything followed in our day.

Note just four marked characteristics of the healings of Christ and the apostles in contrast with present-day so-called healings. In the New Testament the healings, on the whole, were:

1. Instantaneous, not gradual: Luke 4:39; 5:25; 8:47; 18:43; John 5:9; Acts 3:7, 8; 9:34.[1]

2. Complete, not partial: Matthew 14:35, 36; John 7:23; Acts 4:9, 10.

3. Lasting, not momentary: Luke 8:2, 3; John 5:10, 14, 15; Acts 4:14.

4. All-inclusive, not selective: Matthew 9:35; 10:1; 12:15; 15:30, 31; Luke 4:40; 6:17-19; Acts 5:16.[2]

What a far cry these are from what is witnessed in present-day centers of healing!

When we see the type of miraculous healing which conforms to these Biblical standards being freely performed around us, then we will be ready to stop, take note and acknowledge that apparently the New Testament pattern is being complied with. But not until then.

NO POSITIVE OR UNIFORM DIRECTIVES

The Scripture passages presumed to give us reason to expect healing have no direct and unequivocal witness to that end. It has been observed that each text cited refers either to something limited to a particular time and place, to the healing of the soul from sin, or to that which is not set forth for common practice.

Focusing on the New Testament, where some uniform instruction in the matter should be expected, the thrust of each passage calling for attention was seen to be quite different. For example, many claim that God gives certain individuals a special "gift of healing" for the benefit of the faithful, just as He calls certain ones to the ministry of the Word or to missionary service. Yet in only one place is a gift (or rather "gifts") of healing referred to (1 Cor. 12). This, upon examination, was found to set forth no clear injunction for us today.

Again, the anointing with oil for healing is mentioned only in the early epistle of James (chapter 5). The passage basically points up the importance of patience amid afflictions and the privilege of prayer by believers in the face of peculiar needs.

Peter's statement, "By his stripes ye were healed" applied the atonement to the soul. It appears to have no reference to bodily healing or physical needs.

The various statements believed to be relevant are characterized by a wide diversity of thought. Matters of instruction for the people of God throughout the Christian era should not lack pointedness or display such want of consistent testimony.

In Matthew 8 the writer calls attention to Jesus' earthly activity before the cross, in reference to which the Old Testament prophet said He "bare our sicknesses," sympathetically encompassing human need.

In John 14 Jesus said "greater works" than He did would be done. These are works of the Spirit.

Acts 10:38 is simply a declaration of what Jesus did, "healing all that were oppressed of the devil." It is not proof that all bodily sickness is of Satan and has been overcome.

Romans 8:11 says that "your mortal bodies" will be "quickened" (made alive or raised), which we happily look forward to.

Hebrews 13:8 is a matter-of-fact statement that Jesus in His essential being is "the same yesterday, and to day, and for ever."

Where, amid all this, is any coherent basis for a doctrine of healing? Doctrines must be built upon firmer foundations. For either an important belief or practice, something more conclusive should emerge from the infallible record.

FACING IT

The task we set before us is completed. We have examined the leading Bible references upon which the claims of divine healing—as popularly known—are presumed to rest. In passing, some inescapable principles were observed which, if candidly faced, would resolve the question of bodily healing. We have seen that it is impossible to apply consistently specific promises in particular—or the work of Christ generally—to physical healing.

The prominent passages of Scripture touching the subject (studied in the light of the context and recognized principles of Bible interpretation) have been found to be either limited in scope or to say something quite different from what has been supposed. They afford no warrant for claiming immunity from sickness or unfailing healing after illness strikes.

A professed Biblical basis for physical healing can be found apparently only by sidestepping or pitifully twisting the teaching of the Word of God. The challenge remains for sincere and honest people to face this and not to go on statements pressed beyond their evident intent or on a mustering of half-truths.

RECAPITULATION AND RELATED OBSERVATIONS

It may be helpful to put down some observations which can be kept in mind in relation to the broader aspects of this study.

1. God desires and expects faith on the part of His children. Yet faith must be in the right object, or rather in the right Person. It must be in resignation to the perfect divine will. To demand by faith what is beyond this is sheer presumption.

2. It is good to "lay claim" to great things from the Lord,

but such claims must be based upon the clear teaching of the Word of God. Rather than "lay claim" to some much desired benefit, it is better to lay claim to a definite promise of Scripture which is within the scope of what God sets before us.

3. There is no doubt about God's power and ability to heal the body and heal it instantly and completely if He so desires. We also have assurance of God's wisdom and love and that in the long-range aspect of things He knows what is best for His children.

4. On occasion God does heal in answer to prayer scripturally offered and grounded in Christ. Such recoveries from sickness are often well-nigh miraculous.

5. Let it be emphasized that we should pray for the sick. All of our burdens should be taken to the Lord. Included in this are bodily afflictions. Having access to the throne of grace, one should commit body, soul and spirit to the Lord. We should pray for daily bread and for bodily well-being.

6. God is not obligated to heal anyone, nor does He always heal His children. His chastisements may take the form of physical suffering (Heb. 12:5-11; 1 Cor. 11:30). Even when not coming as chastisement, God may allow His choicest servants to suffer (Heb. 11:36-39; 2 Cor. 12:7-10).

7. It pleases God to heal sometimes with means (medicines or common remedies), sometimes without means, sometimes not at all.

8. Some of the most godly and devout Christians the world has known were weak in body and even chronic invalids, and yet they possessed a faith in God that shamed many a physically robust believer.

9. Thousands of Christians who never make any claim to divine healing are strong and active, even down to old age. On the other hand a large number of those who profess divine healing and are ever claiming it never seem to have it.

10. Some who have recovered from sickness and have attributed it to a miraculous occurrence or to a faith ministry may actually have gotten well as a result of the natural processes operative in their bodies. Or they may have been graciously cured entirely apart from the ministration to which they attribute it.

11. It appears that many so-called miraculous healings result from the emotional release found in fervent "revival" meetings. Many apparent cures come from the effects of mass psychology (often near hysteria) where crowds are skillfully manipulated.

12. The promoters of bodily healing may be true to the faith and preach a worthy salvation gospel. But they err in certain respects. Souls may be truly converted under such preaching, but they may fall into error either under the teaching of those from whom they first heard the gospel or elsewhere.

13. We ask candidly, Would the most confident believer in divine healing seriously look to God to replace an amputated limb or a missing eye? God could do so in an instant; nothing is impossible to Him. But does He do so, or are these things His will for us?[3]

14. If it is proper to wash the outside of the body with soap and water for the healthful benefit derived therefrom, why not cleanse the throat, for example, with an appropriate cleansing gargle to wash it of germs acquired from our contaminated environment? Should we discard the use of toothpaste and claim complete dental well-being on the basis of God's power to heal? Are the uses of mechanical exercisers evidence of lack of faith? If a medical cure is out, is the manicure also? Where is one to stop?

15. Wonderful testimonials are frequently given in behalf of the benefits of patent medicines, health-rejuvenating products and various nostrums. These things may or may not have benefited their users. A testimonial alone is no proof of either a scientific basis of effectiveness or of divine intervention in behalf of the one making the claim. For the former (medical measures), its chief benefit may derive from the user's confidence in it; for the latter (divine working), a sound scriptural basis must underlie it.

16. Those with ample means may resort to the mountains where they can benefit from a change of air, or they may embark on a sea voyage with its relaxing and invigorating potential. Their poorer fellows might be told that it is a lack of faith when they resort to some less expensive medical remedy in attempting to improve a similar bodily condition.

17. Even a verified "faith healing" would be no absolute proof that God was at work in the channel employed or in the agency to which credit is given. Christian Science claims hundreds of authentic cases of healing. We do not deny that in some instances real recoveries may be among these. Neither do we have the final word in explaining them. The same may be said in regard to healings at Roman Catholic shrines. We simply point out that virtually none of these conform to the Biblical standard.

18. The so-called faith healers exhibit nothing which is superior to what is claimed by pagan witch doctors, voodoo enchanters, black magic operators, spiritists, clairvoyant workers, mind-over-matter practitioners, hypnotists, or those endeavoring to employ ancient or revived exorcism. Results have come from these, but the child of God should rigidly shun such channels, as dire dangers lurk within them.

19. God wants His children to bear testimony to the world, not in the sense of escaping all the inconveniences of the world (in that case He would have removed them at once from it), but in courageously bearing up under its afflictions. It would be impossible for Christians to be sustained amid suffering if there were no suffering Christians to prove God's grace to them. There would never have been any martyr spirit if there had never been any martyrs to display it.

20. In the wilderness the Children of Israel received the manna directly from God. But that was merely a temporary arrangement. Later they were taught that the fruits of the land, for which they had to struggle, were just as truly from God as was the manna. They could see in this nonmiraculous supply God's perfect provision for them. Why did not the almighty and all-loving God continue to undertake in miraculous ways to provide for His children?

21. As a result of Christ's complete atonement, the child of God will someday be "delivered from the bondage of corruption" (Rom. 8:21). A glorious day is coming when sickness and pain will be known no more, when the redeemed in their resurrection bodies shall enjoy perfect health and every aspect of well-being.

LEAVING IT WITH GOD

Having said that God can and on occasion does answer prayer for bodily healing, let God's people praise Him when it is granted. And let them humbly bow to His sovereign will when the answer is not that which may have been desired.

We wish we could hold out unfailing hope to all who are suffering physically. But one cannot go beyond what the Word of God holds out. We are not unsympathetic to those with deep needs. Why a God of infinite love allows some to suffer is a matter beyond any of us. It touches the larger subject of the problem of human suffering on which much of value has already been written.

We know that God is good. We also know that He desires His children to exemplify faith and confidence. May we trust Him even when we cannot understand and leave ourselves in His all-wise hands.

TRIUMPHANT TESTIMONIES

A godly pastor was faithfully serving his church in a central European parish when fire destroyed what he had, along with most of the town. This was followed by bereavement which took the good man's family. Then paralysis left him blind and a helpless cripple. After these accumulated afflictions, before he died in 1737, Benjamin Schmolke dictated from his bed the hymn which has been sung around the world:

> My Jesus, as Thou wilt;
>   Oh, may Thy will be mine;
> Into Thy hand of love
>   I would my all resign:
> Through sorrow or through joy,
>   Conduct me as Thine own,
> And help me still to say,
>   My Lord, Thy will be done!
>
> My Jesus, as Thou wilt;
>   Though seen through many a tear,
> Let not my star of hope
>   Grow dim or disappear:

> Since Thou on earth hast wept,
> And sorrowed oft alone,
> If I must weep with Thee,
> My Lord, Thy will be done.

Another who suffered poor health was Elizabeth Prentiss, but she saw God's purposes in such ills. Before her death from a lingering illness, she asked for an increase in grief and pain so that she could have greater love for Christ.

> Let sorrow do its work,
> Send grief and pain;
> Sweet are Thy messengers,
> Sweet their refrain,
> When they can sing with me:
> More love, O Christ, to Thee,
> More love to Thee.

It was my privilege to visit Martha Snell Nicholson shortly before her death. Nearly all her life she was an invalid. Her emaciated frame was grotesquely contorted by arthritis from which she suffered for years. to say nothing of tuberculosis, ankylosed spine, angina, Parkinson's disease and finally cancer. Her radiant testimony and undimmed love for the Savior put me to shame. Her volumes of deeply moving poems, having gone through many editions, have blessed multitudes. She speaks out of deep personal experience when she says,

> As was its wont, my day began with pain,
> The old familiar suffering again;
> And yet, because my day began with prayer,
> I bore no pain alone—my Lord was there.

> My day began with weakness, I was spent;
> But if I ever wondered what it meant,
> He showed me, ere the day had reached its length;
> My weakness was made perfect in His strength!

Then, even more fully explaining her close personal experience with suffering:

> I stood, a mendicant of God
> Before His royal throne,

And begged Him for one priceless gift
   For me to call my own.

I took the gift from out His hand,
   But as I would depart
I cried, "But, Lord, this is a thorn
   And it doth pierce my heart.

This is a strange and hurtful gift
   Which Thou hast given me."
He said, "Nay, child, I give good gifts;
   And gave My best to thee."

I took it home, and though at first
   The cruel thorn hurt sore,
As long years passed I grew at last
   To love it more and more.

I learned He never gives a thorn
   Without this added grace:
He takes the thorn to pin aside
   The veil which hides His face!

A CLOSING WORD

A tragic outgrowth of unfounded claims that healing today should be found in the atonement is that when sincere individuals have sought that healing and it has failed them, doubts are cast upon all of Christ's work. Not only may dark clouds of discouragement and depression come over one as a result of not finding for the body that which supposedly should be found, but the soul's whole relation to Christ is thereby cast in doubt.

Many advocates of bodily healing give the impression that the physical is the outstanding thing. This is a great error in our day—putting the emphasis on the material and the temporal. Rather, the condition of the soul far outweighs anything affecting the body. The emphasis should be placed on the forgiveness of sin and salvation rather than on mere physical well-being. That was the main purpose of Christ's advent into the world and the paramount goal of His work on our behalf. The familiar lines put it rightly:

> To lose your wealth is much,
> To lose your health is more,
> To lose your soul is such a loss
> That nothing can restore.

The benefit to the soul will last forever, and as a by-product, it will assure all other rightful blessings.

NOTES:

1. In two of Jesus' healing miracles there may be a question if what took place was instantaneous. However, in both of these exceptional cases the ones concerned were completely healed within the very hour they were dealt with, and they were healed in immediate steps with nothing intervening. Both cases involved blindness. The process Christ used either encouraged faith or illustrated that often the blindness of men's hearts may be progressively removed. The notable thing in each miracle, however, was that the Lord did not leave any man with a partial recovery, as is so often done nowadays. He brought to completion whatever He undertook to do.

In the first case, Mark 8:22-26, Jesus touched the blind man twice. But within a matter of minutes, complete healing resulted. In the second case, John 9:1-7, He placed clay over the blind man's eyes. Of course there was no full sight until he had washed it away. Again, it was such a sudden and complete healing that it was a marvel to all who heard of it (vv. 8 ff).

In the healing recorded in John 4:46-54 are the words "he began to amend" (v. 52), speaking of the nobleman's son. This is not the gospel writer's comment on the incident; this is the question asked by the nobleman—the naturalistic point of view. The answer to that question indicated specifically the very "hour the fever left him" (v. 52).

It is said of a centurion's servant whom Jesus healed that he "was healed in the selfsame hour" (Matt. 8:13). The Amplified Version renders it, "at that very moment"; Berkeley, "at that exact moment"; Weymouth, "precisely at that time"; and the Twentieth Century New Testament, "that very instant."

2. Mark 6:5 and 6, Matthew 13:58 record that Jesus could not do many "mighty works" because of unbelief; He healed only "a few" of the sick. The reference is to the town of Nazareth where Jesus spent His boyhood. Having seen Him grow up as a common carpenter, they

resented His having forsaken His hometown for other places in which to do great works. Accordingly, they rejected the superlative nature of His very person. Their unbelief went beyond what applied anywhere else. He was the prophet without honor in his own country. Thus where few believed, few would seek Him out—thereby affording Him but little opportunity to do many mighty works in that particular place.

3. An account has come to my attention which claims that an eye which was accidentally torn out and destroyed was miraculously replaced. We wish the details could be verified. Maybe someone will come forth with the testimony of a severed limb restored. If that is likely, why not the heads of courageous saints who were beheaded for their faith? It reminds me of a clipping from a Manila, Philippines, newspaper. A community was finishing the construction of the image of the patron saint. The prelate decreed that a dog's blood would be appropriate for the painting of the image. A dog was seized, its head cut off, and its blood so used. The head and carcass were thrown into the nearby river, whereupon the head and body came together, and the dog swam to the shore and trotted up to its master. The miracle was said to have occurred as evidence of the saint's pleasure in the sacrifice which was made.

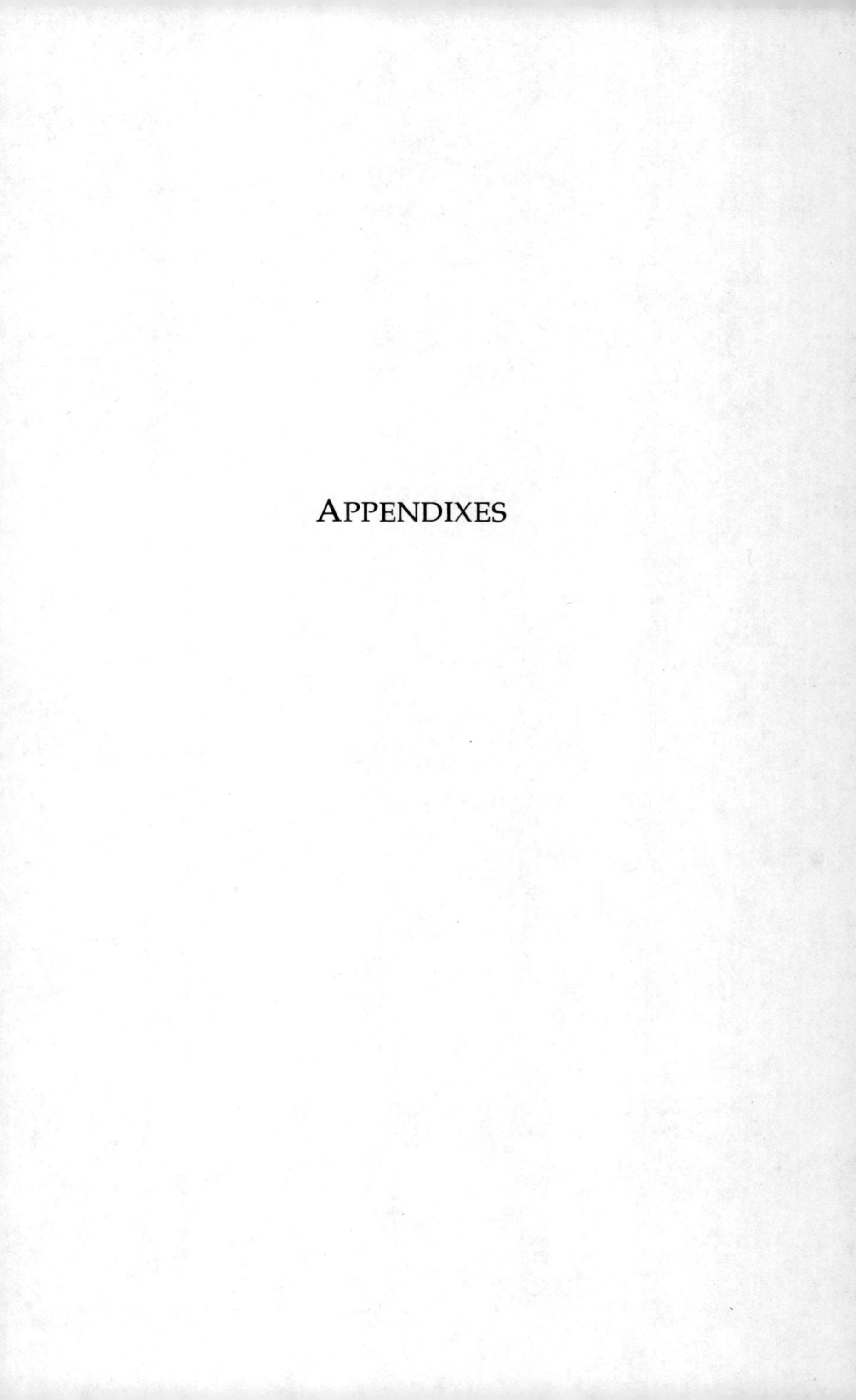

APPENDIXES

Appendix A

Miracles and Commonly Recurring Events

In recent days it has become popular among charismatics and others to talk much about miracles. "I believe in miracles," is the cry; or, "God can perform a miracle for you"; or, "Ask God for a miracle." The term *miracle* seems to fascinate people. They want to prate about miracles, claim their occurrence, or point to where they are said to be taking place.

It is commonly asserted that miracle works are ever available to those who have faith to appropriate them. But miracles, if exercised as a regular thing among people, would by that regularity cease to be miraculous. Much confusion relative to miraculous divine healing obtains here.

What is a miracle? *Webster's New Collegiate Dictionary* (eighth edition) defines a miracle "an extraordinary event . . . an extremely outstanding or unusual event." Its being extraordinary or unusual would thus preclude its being commonly repeated or regularly occurring. Therefore, to say that miracles may regularly take place among us is a confusion of terms. A miracle in the physical realm might be defined as something deviating from the ordinary or known laws of nature. If they commonly occur, such occurrences would establish a new principle of operation. This new law would take them out of the sphere of what is properly designated a miracle.

William E. Gladstone, the eminent four-time prime minister of England, who was interested in and wrote on religious themes, recognized this principle: "If the experience of miracles were universal, they would cease to be miracles" (quoted by Anderson, *The Silence of God*, p. 30).

The scholarly American, B. B. Warfield, says, "If miracles are to be common, every-day occurrences, normal and not extraordinary, they cease to attract attention, and lose their very reason of existence. What is normal is according to law. If miracles are the law of the Christian life they cease to serve their chief end" (*Counterfeit Miracles*, p. 193).

Another Britisher, Robert Tuck, similarly points out: "Miracles must in their very nature be temporary. As soon as the things which we call miracles become permanent and regular, they come into the natural order, and cease to be surprises. We are familiar with them, and they no longer bear testimony to us of Divine interferences" (*A Handbook of Biblical Difficulties*, p. 514).

Luther T. Townsend put it in an interesting way: "If the Creator's goodness were such as to lead him to keep interfering with the law of gravitation lest careless men should break their necks while falling from a building, the whole planetary system, by that same interference might be plunged into confusion. The wreck of a railway train in which a hundred passengers are killed and maimed . . . [is] appalling . . . but if it result from the execution of natural law, there is this compensation: that confidence in natural law is established. . . . It appears, therefore, that God's goodness would not be manifested so much by constant interference with the operation of his laws, even to save life and prevent suffering, as by their rigorous enforcement" (*God's Goodness and Severity*, pp. 119, 120).

Some maintain that through Christ's work all sickness has been paid for and that deliverance from infirmities should ever be expected by God's people. They assert that these healings are miracles, real miracles. Logically speaking, it could only be one way or the other: something commonly happening and not a miracle, or miraculous and an unusual event. These matters should be so designated as to convey consistently the position assumed.

A British scholar describes a miracle as "a strange and unusual event, which we cannot account for . . . specially worked by God. . . . In the New Testament the words used are *wonders, mighty works,* and *signs.*" Then this writer says, "We have no right to pray for *miracles . . .* though we have a right to pray for an ordinary event, such as rain or recovery from sickness. . . . In the Bible miracles were sometimes prayed for, but only by persons who acted under Divine guidance; and this affords no argument for our doing so" (W. H. Turton, *The Truth of Christianity* [New York: G. P. Putnam's Sons, 1910], pp. 116, 117, 522, 523).

The word *miracle* in the common English Bible is a very loose rendering of either of two terms in the original, the words being *power* (or mighty work) and *sign* (attesting sign). Neither of these is translated from the Greek in a majority of its appearances as "miracle." A thoroughly consistent translation, therefore, would eliminate entirely the word *miracle* from Scripture. But even using the more accurate renderings, it cannot be established that either *powers* or *signs* became commonplace, except in the ministry of our Lord who was Himself the miracle *par excellence.* (For distinctions in the New Testament terms involved, see R. C. Trench, *Synonyms of the New Testament,* section 91.)

Miracles in the recognized dictionary meaning of the term did occur as recorded in Scripture, but being extraordinary and unusual, no general pattern of regularity in respect to them can be established. Indeed, Jesus Himself indicated that they were the exception. He said, "Many widows were in Israel in the days of [Elijah] . . . when great famine was throughout all the land; But unto none of them was [Elijah] sent, save . . . unto a woman that was a widow. And many lepers were in Israel in the time of [Elisha] the prophet; and none of them was cleansed, saving Naaman the Syrian" (Luke 4:25-27). Miracles, then, should be recognized as out of the ordinary and not as something to be commonly expected.

While not the rule, however, a true miracle may yet take place on occasion as it may please God to grant something special. At any rate we should remember—miracle or not—God is still mighty to answer prayer.

Appendix B

A Healing Philosophy
of Subtiler Dimensions

A philosophy of healing is coming forward which may seem to be on a higher level. It embraces the idea that between the inner and the outer man are reciprocal influences. Since the gospel is for the "whole person," the physical will benefit from readjustments in other areas. Restoring "wholeness" to the entire person clears away resentments, frustrations, hidden guilt complexes and the like which are claimed to be the basic and deeper causes of ill health. Letting God take over, the thinking runs, is intended to remove these blocks to spiritual well-being, thereby bringing mental, emotional and even physical restoration.

The literature of this school of thought is replete with impressive accounts of those who, after having underlying hindrances removed, found the entire man restored, including physical healing. Medical authorities are freely cited, acknowledging the limitations of materia medica to bring about cures when the patient's need of spiritual and psychical uplift is essential to bodily recovery.

We do not deny a large element of truth in this. Certainly, deep resentments, long smoldering conflicts, inner tensions and the like may well underlie much physical suffering. Their removal often brings notable organic relief. But such personal needs cannot be said to be the cause of ills such as those brought about by injuries or those whose source is infection. In these cases healing cannot be effected by spiritual treatment.

Our appeal has been to the primacy of Scripture. Therefore we ask, Where is any direct Biblical basis for saying that bodily recovery is to follow or be included in changed attitudes or the clearing up of frustrations? Indeed, where in Scripture are such elements as inner tensions, mental or spiritual blocks, personal resentments or the like referred to or dealt with by any Biblical character as a means to physical cures? Jesus and the apostles never told anyone that if these things were cleared away, physical healing would spontaneously follow.

No psychological blocks to "wholeness" would have been responsible for afflictions such as leprosy; or for one crippled "from his mother's womb" (Acts 3:2-8; 14:8-10); or for the man born blind (John 9:1-7). In this latter case, not even the parents could be held responsible (vv. 2, 3). It would have been uncalled for to expect healing by adjustments in "the total person."

Reading the literature of this spreading philosophy reveals that a gospel is emphasized which centers in the temporal existence of its subjects. The here-on-earth aspect of one's life is given the priority. Notably lacking is recognition that every soul passing through life has a final Hell to avoid as well as a Heaven to gain. Some would be shocked by the mention of these things. They ignore the judicial aspect of sin's guilt before a holy God, Who will mete out just judgment on all. Mental and physical benefits are stressed in dealing with souls. Individuals do not face sin's eternal consequences. It is a false kindness of tragic proportions to help one with temporal benefits and then leave that one to perish everlastingly. Is the spiritual need denied, or is it assumed to take care of itself when this life's welfare is met? This is not the teaching of the Word of God!

Appendix C

A Point of Christian Service

After all that has gone before, a brief word may be addressed to those who would be of service to their distressed fellow human beings. Sufferers are all around us, and they desperately need a bit of sympathy and a word which will point them to a firm source of comfort and hope. This area merits serious consideration.

As to regular hospital visitation, more and more only those with special qualifications or training will be recognized for such continuous ministry. But any concerned child of God will find opportunities to display sympathy, share the burden and give spiritual comfort to the sick and afflicted about him.

Pastoral training courses give consideration to the minister's responsibility in visiting the sick and dealing with the suffering. A number of works have been published on the subject of ministry to the sick, the pastor's visit to the sick and counseling the distressed. Shorter treatment of these matters is usually found in minister's handbooks. But anyone can share the stabilizing influence of Scripture and the hope of the gospel with those going through deep water.

Seminars and clinical institutes are held on occasion to encourage and train Christian workers to minister to the afflicted. It is vital that a spiritual, scriptural approach be pursued. Approaches purely along psychological lines do not of themselves give a complete answer. It is even less called for and often disastrous to insist that the afflicted exercise faith in miracle works. The balanced teaching of the Word of God needs to be recognized and followed.

Through wise and Spirit-led counseling, one in real need may be led to throw off or overcome debilitating effects of frustrations, resentments, jealousy, a sense of insufficiency, of failure, loss of self-esteem, guilt complexes, fears of the past, of the unknown, and the like—any of which can be reflected in bodily states.

Those who would help the suffering should not neglect the fruitful service field of ministering to persons in real need. This is only a part of Christian charity incumbent upon those with a heart of compassion. We should all bear one another's burdens and so fulfill the law of Christ. The least to be expected is that one show sympathy, kindly interest and a desire to understand what the sick may be passing through. Prayer is always in order, and it should be offered, not in a mere professional manner or as a passing duty, but with earnestness and a consciousness that the Lord's ear is indeed open to the cry of His children and that His consolations exceed anything that the world can offer.

BIBLIOGRAPHY

Anderson, Sir Robert. *The Silence of God.* Grand Rapids: Kregel Publications, 1952.

Biederwolf, William E. *Whipping-Post Theology.* Grand Rapids: William B. Eerdmans, 1934.

Bingham, Rowland V. *The Bible and the Body.* Toronto: Evangelical Publishers, 1921.

Boggs, Wade H., Jr. *Faith Healing and the Christian Faith.* Richmond: John Knox Press, 1956.

Bruce, Alexander B. *The Miraculous Element in the Gospels.* London: Hodder & Stoughton, 1902.

Bruce, F. F. *Answers to Questions.* Grand Rapids: Zondervan Publishing House, 1972.

Conybeare, W. J. and J. S. Howson. *The Life and Epistles of St. Paul.* New York: Charles Scribner & Co., 1869.

Fisher, George Park. *The Grounds of Theistic and Christian Belief.* London: Hodder & Stoughton, 1908.

Frank, Jerome D. *Persuasion and Healing: A Comparative Study of Psychotherapy.* Baltimore: The Johns Hopkins Press, 1961.

Gaebelein, Arno C. *The Healing Question.* New York: Our Hope Publication Office, 1925.

Hagen, Kristofer. *Faith and Health.* Philadelphia: Muhlenberg Press, 1961.

Lange, John Peter. *Commentary on the Holy Scriptures: II Timothy*. Grand Rapids: Zondervan Publishing House, n.d.

Moule, Handley C. G. *Veni Creator*. London: Pickering and Inglis, n.d.

Pierson, Arthur T. *George Muller of Bristol*. New York: Loizeaux Brothers, 1944.

Pink, Arthur W. *Divine Healing*. Swengel, PA: Reiner Publications, n.d.

Rackham, Richard B. *The Acts of the Apostles*. London: Methuen & Co., 1953.

Reed, Louis S. *The Healing Cults*. Chicago: The University of Chicago Press, 1932.

Robertson, A. T. *Word Pictures in the New Testament*, Vol. VI. Nashville: Broadman Press, n.d.

Scroggie, W. Graham. *Speaking with Tongues*. New York: The Book Stall, 1919.

Trench, Richard C. *Notes on the Miracles of Our Lord*. Grand Rapids: Baker Book House, 1968.

Tuck, Robert. *A Handbook of Biblical Difficulties*. New York: Thomas Whittaker, 1888.

Turton, W. H. *The Truth of Christianity*. New York: G. P. Putnam's Sons, 1910.

Warfield, Benjamin B. *Counterfeit Miracles*. New York: Charles Scribner's Sons, 1918.

SCRIPTURE INDEX